AFRICAN TEXTILES

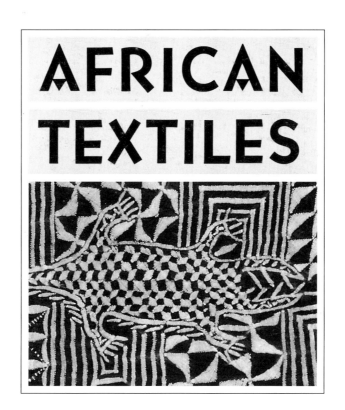

AFRICAN
TEXTILES

JOHN PICTON & JOHN MACK

Published for the
Trustees of the British Museum
by British Museum Press

Third impression 1993

Published by British Museum Press
A division of British Museum Publications Ltd
46 Bloomsbury Street, London WC1B 3QQ

British Library Cataloguing in Publication Data

Picton, John
African textiles. – 2nd ed.
1. African textile arts
I. Title   II. Mack, John   III. British Museum
746'.096

ISBN 0-7141-1595-9

First edition published 1979
ISBN 0-7141-1552-5 cased
ISBN 0-7141-1553-3 paper

Designed by Harry Green

Set in Palatino by Tradespools
and printed in Hong Kong

Cover Detail of the patterning on a silk and cotton hammock, Ewe, Ghana. 1981. Af 13.1.

Page 1 Detail from resist-dyed cotton cloth, Igbo, Nigeria. See also p. 151.

Pages 2–3 Cut-pile raphia textile, Kuba, Zaire. See also p. 197.

CONTENTS

PREFACE

Amodu Ihiovi of Opopocho village near Okene, Ebira, Nigeria, wearing his best gown of red, yellow and pale blue cotton with dark green silk embroidery.

When preparing the first edition of *African Textiles* ten years ago we had two audiences in mind. One was those people with established interests in textiles, yet who knew little about Africa and its weaving practice; the other was those with experience of Africa, but little knowledge of weaving. As we wrote, this audience more or less defined itself. We were then jointly responsible for the African collections of the British Museum's Department of Ethnography at the Museum of Mankind, and our most consistent inquiries about textiles came from these sources. The book was thus, to an extent, a response to public interest.

It is gratifying to realise that in the time since we first worked on this book it has continued to be in regular demand and to be widely cited by colleagues as a useful introduction. This is especially encouraging because a large exhibition that it originally accompanied has since closed, although nearly all of the material exhibited was drawn from the British Museum's extensive collection and remains accessible. The exhibition was shown at the Museum of Mankind between late 1979 and 1982 and subsequently transferred in 1983 for a six-month period to the American Museum of Natural History in New York.

In the years that have elapsed interest in the subject has grown steadily, and much further work has been published. Particularly important is the fact that a great deal of this has been based on original fieldwork which has extended our appreciation of the subject. In this second edition of *African Textiles* we intended, therefore, to try and take advantage of these developments where they suggest the need to extend or, in some cases, alter the content of the original book. Sometimes the new information that has become available is sufficiently innovative and comprehensive that, without greatly extending the text, we have been able to do little more than refer the reader to the new sources. To this end the major publications involved are listed in an expanded bibliography.

In addition, both of us have, in the interim, had the opportunity to carry out our own further field research (John Picton in Nigeria in 1981 and 1982), and John Mack on the island of Madagascar in 1984, 1985 and 1987). Although neither of us was working specifically and exclusively on the subject of textiles, the occasion none the less allowed us to pursue this interest and to gather further information which we have incorporated here. In the case of Madagascar no substantial study of its weaving technologies had been published in English when the first edition of this book was in preparation, and indeed very little was available in any other language either. One reviewer at the time found that our attempt to summarise in a separate chapter what had already been published over-emphasised the distinctiveness of Malagasy weaving within African practice. With the benefit of fieldwork we now feel, even more strongly, that Madagascar deserves separate treatment and have revised this chapter in the light of our findings more thoroughly than any other.

As we read through our original text, a number of points struck us forcibly. We feel now, as we did before, that the subject of textiles would benefit from a major discussion of indigenous interpretation of pattern, of pattern names, and of the contexts within which different categories of cloth are used. As anthropologists this is also one of our own interests. It would, however, make this a quite different book if we were to seek to include detailed consideration of these subjects here. As historians of art we realise, too, just how little any of us knows about the creative and aesthetic motivations of the artists concerned, or about the historical processes that have shaped the textile traditions we see now.

For these reasons we are as reluctant as before to enter into debate on the history and diffusion of weaving technologies in Africa. While, at the simplest, the distribution of different technological refinements can readily be mapped, guessing at the circumstances which led to particular distributions can never be more than an interesting parlour game unless many other types of evidence are assembled in support. Knowledge of the functional and temporal relationships between the relevant variables (technology, weave structures, the economic bases, and so forth) is still not sufficient to permit anything more.

On the other hand, we found our original references to 'traditional' weaving practice in Africa and to the continent's 'traditional' textiles confusing. What we intended, of course, was to contrast local non-industrial production with the technologically sophisticated textile industries which some African countries have been able to develop, or the imported cloth that is widely marketed. It is all too easy, however, to imply as a result that tradition is a static and unchanging phenomenon, particularly when this technology is compared with the evolutions in industrial processes. In Nigeria, however, the dazzling effects of lurex have been extensively exploited in modern times by 'traditional' weavers; in Madagascar the loom used to weave a silk burial shroud also produces a thick blanket with a warp composed of stripped plastic and a weft of rags knotted together. These are but two instances in our own recent experience of contemporary developments of a kind that could equally be duplicated in historical times.

We could hardly reject Asante silk weaving, or the colonial imagery of some Yoruba *adire* cloths, on the grounds that they are not 'traditional'. The easy acceptance of the supposed category, 'traditional art', is in effect a denial of the temporal and creative dynamic embedded in particular traditions. Contemporary developments in local textile practices enable a salutary corrective. For these reasons we have endeavoured to clarify the sense of our original text; and we have, we hope, given due attention to lurex in the additional illustrations we have been able to include.

ACKNOWLEDGEMENTS

Several people outside the British Museum have assisted in the gathering together of information for this book. We should like to thank in particular James Bynon, Margret Carey, the Revd J. T. Hardyman, Bruce Kent, Alastair and Venice Lamb, Len Pole and Nancy Stanfield.

Photographs by Keith Nicklin, John Picton and Susan Picton are reproduced by kind permission of Dr Ekpo Eyo, at the time of the first edition, Director-General of the National Commission for Museums and Monuments, Nigeria, to whom grateful thanks are also due for the opportunities to carry out field research in that country.

The authors and publishers are grateful to the following for permission to reproduce photographs:

Philip Allison 44, 109; Peter Andrews 56; Basel Mission 167 *above*; Maurice Bloch 135 *above*, 136; R. E. Bradbury 14 *right*, 178 *right*; Jean Brown 95; James Byron 15 *far right*, 21, 22, 26, 27, 28, 29, 58 *both*, 59, 60 *top right*, *bottom left and right*, 64, 184 *above*; William Fagg 80–1; Bruce Kent 39, 40, 41 *both*, 42; Venice and Alastair Lamb 10, 46, 48, 101, 106, 115 *both*, 117, 120, 121, 127, 192 *left*; Elizabeth McClelland 36, 76; John Mack 132 *all*, 134; Malcolm McLeod 119; Musée Royale de l'Afrique Centrale, Tervuren 19, 47, 84 *both*, 85, 86, 88, 175 *above*, 184 *below*; Keith Nicklin and Jill Salmons 33, 34, 179; Robert Osoba (courtesy Jane Barbour) 37; Charles Partridge 177, 180; Otto Peetz Collection 140; John Picton 6, 13 *above right*, 14 *above*, 16 *above*, 20, 30 *right*, 69 *all*, 71 *above right*, 72, 73, 75 *above*, 92, 94 *above*, 193 *above*; Susan Picton 30 *left*, 31, 168, 172; Major P. H. G. Powell-Cotton 183 *below*; C. G. Seligman 54; Doig Simmonds 154 *below*; Nancy Stanfield 38, 94 *below*, 116, 148 *left*, 152, 155 *above*, *centre*, 158, 159; Emil Torday 13 *above*; The Trustees of the British Museum 16 *below*, 17, 35, 57 *below*, *right*, 61, 62–3, 65, 66, 71 *left*, *below*, 74, 75 *below*, 78–9, 82, 89, 90, 91, 97, 98, 99 *both*, 100, 102–3, 104, 107, 110 *both*, 111, 114, 118, 122–3, 124, 125, 126, 128, 129, 130, 138–9, 141, 142, 143, 144, 146, 148 *right*, 149 *both*, 150 *both*, 151, 153 *both*, 154 *above*, 155 *below right*, 156, 157 *both*, 160, 162, 164, 165, 166, 167 *below*, 170, 171 *both*, 173, 174, 175 *below*, 176, 178 *left*, 181, 182, 183 *above*, 185, 186, 188, 192 *right*, 193 *below*, 194, 195, 196 *both*, 197, 198, 199, 200, 201

The line drawings are by Ben Burt and the maps by Technical Art Services.

CHAPTER ONE

INTRODUCTION

A man of importance of the Ewe people, south-eastern Ghana. The cloth is woven in strips about 4 in (10 cm) wide sewn together edge to edge. The design is an extremely fine example of pattern carried entirely in the weft.

One of the most obvious features of the material culture of Africa is cloth. Woven textiles, and other fabrics, are available in almost every part of the continent, and more often than not in substantial quantity. This is, of course, particularly apparent in any market in West or North Africa; but it is surely hardly less true of other regions. As far as the textiles are concerned, some of these fabrics will be imported from Europe and India, though by the present time the greater part is likely to be locally manufactured. Of this, much will be the product of industrial equipment and processes in the factories of post-colonial Africa; and yet much will have come from the hands of spinners, weavers and dyers still working, and very often flourishing, within the traditions of pre-colonial origin that continue to be of cultural and social relevance, with a secure indigenous patronage. These provide the subject matter of this book.

Textiles as a context of culture

The most obvious use of textiles is as articles of clothing. One or more lengths of cloth may be draped around the body, or tailored to make gowns, tunics, trousers and so on. Modesty, whatever that may mean to a particular people, and protection against the elements are, however, not the only purposes of clothing. Particular colours or decorative embellishments or shapes of garment may have cultural value such that the wearer is immediately associated with the possession of great wealth or status. Alternatively, an otherwise relatively poor man may possess one costly gown which he will wear only at important occasions.

Particular colours, kinds of decoration or shapes of garment may also have political or ritual significances. The tribal affiliation of a Moroccan Berber woman, for example, can be seen (coincidentally) in the pattern of stripes of her cloak. In Benin, Nigeria, chiefs wear red cloth as part of their ceremonial court dress; and red by its association with anger, blood, war and fire is regarded as threatening. By the wearing of such cloth a chief protects himself, and his king, from evil, that is to say from witchcraft and from the magical forces employed by their enemies (Paula Ben-Amos, 1977). In addition, however, some chiefs wear red cloth which is scalloped to produce a type of skirt known as 'pangolin skin'. The scales of the pangolin are widely used also as a protective charm against evil and the pangolin is regarded as the one animal the leopard (a metaphor of kingship) cannot kill. Wearing this costume can, in addition to giving protection from evil, be interpreted as referring to the potential opposition between the king and the Town Chiefs, the resolution of which is so important a part of the political tradition in Benin. In this particular case the red cloth used is of

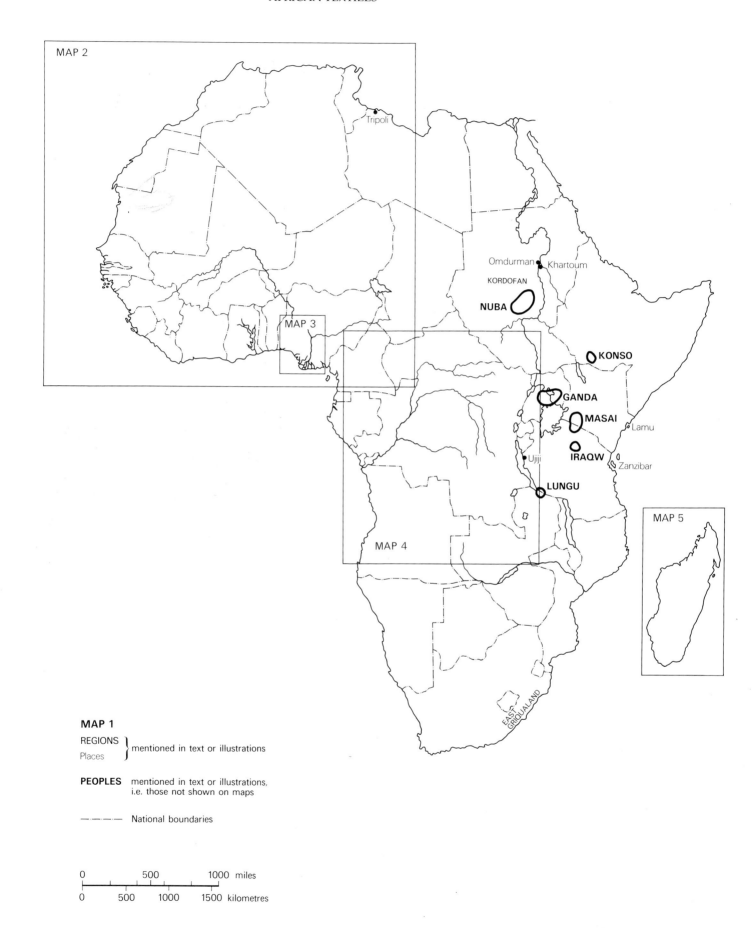

MAP 2

Tripoli

Omdurman • Khartoum

KORDOFAN

NUBA

KONSO

MAP 3

GANDA

MASAI

Lamu

Ujiji

IRAQW

Zanzibar

LUNGU

MAP 4

MAP 5

EAST GRIQUALAND

MAP 1

REGIONS
Places } mentioned in text or illustrations

PEOPLES mentioned in text or illustrations,
i.e. those not shown on maps

—·—·— National boundaries

| 0 | 500 | 1000 | miles |

| 0 | 500 | 1000 | 1500 | kilometres |

Above A man wearing a raphia cloth bordered with raphia buttons. Bunda, Zaire.

Above right Skeins of indigo-dyed yarn for sale in an Akoko-Edo market, Nigeria. The women are wearing as skirts lengths of cotton cloth which they have woven.

Opposite Africa. For areas in rectangles see maps 2–5 on pages 51, 68, 87 and 133.

European manufacture although it has been imported into Benin since the late fifteenth century. (As we shall see, we cannot ignore the use of European products in textile design and manufacture in Africa.)

The basic colour spectrum of Africa, red, black and white, is, of course, rarely without some level of significance although the precise nature of this significance will vary from one people to another. Elsewhere in Nigeria, as among the Ebira for example, red is a colour associated not with danger and war but with success and achievement with which they overlap but do not coincide; and in Madagascar the term 'red', *mena*, is applied to burial cloths though with the sense of 'colourful' rather than because they are dominantly red in colour. The contrast is at least in part between the colourful shrouds of the dead and the white cloth worn by mourners.

Textiles are not only used to clothe the living, obviously, but also the dead (as in the above Malagasy example), as well as providing clothing for the manifestations of the world of the dead, or of some other mode of existence, in masquerade form. Here too colour is likely to be of significance and certain kinds of textile may be produced specifically for such purposes. Textiles may be used to dress neither person, corpse nor spirit, but a house, to mark an event of some significance, or, similarly, a shrine. Finally, gifts of textiles are a means by which social relationships are created and maintained.

In the absence of woven cloth people may use barkcloth or skins, and in a few places

Above A masquerader commemorating a deceased elder. Ebira, Nigeria. The costume is made up of Bunnu red burial cloth, imported for the purpose, together with locally woven shroud cloth. The costume also incorporates relics of the deceased man it commemorates. (The Ebira are close neighbours of the Bunnu.)

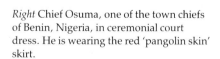

Right Chief Osuma, one of the town chiefs of Benin, Nigeria, in ceremonial court dress. He is wearing the red 'pangolin skin' skirt.

Far right Three young women of the Ayt Brahim, one of the tribes of the Ayt Hadiddu, eastern High Atlas, Morocco. They wear the cloak and headdress proper to women of their tribe.

14

A house dressed for a funeral in a Bunnu-Yoruba village, Nigeria. Inside, the corpse of an important man awaits burial. This is indicated by the distinctive red prestige burial cloths of the area displayed on the roof.

A puppet show in northern Nigeria. The puppeteer's booth is an embroidered, indigo-dyed Hausa gown of the usual wide-sleeved variety. The puppets are displayed through the neck of the gown.

almost the only form of bodily attire is paint. Frequently textiles are worn in combination with non-textile fabrics, skins or paint. The simplest form of West African man's dress, for example, is a triangular leather apron, worn around the waist and sometimes tucked between the legs, together with a length of cloth thrown over one shoulder. Although this book is about textiles rather than about costume, since barkcloth, skins and body decoration are analogous to textiles in some areas and combined with them in others, they cannot be left altogether out of any consideration of the subject.

Cloth is also a marketable commodity and has been the subject of extensive trade within and beyond the continent of Africa. In some places one range of cloths is

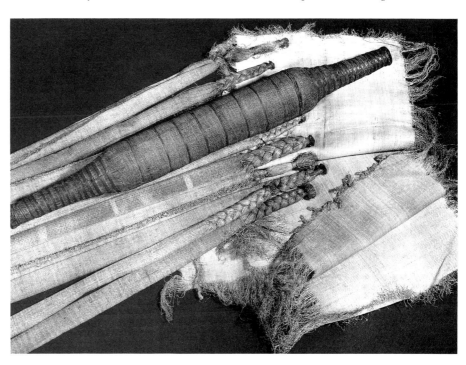

Three types of raphia currency, Zaire. The five small woven squares, which are sewn together at one corner, were collected amongst the Yanzi (+2368). The other types all come from the area occupied by the Bunda (1954 Af 23Q: Wellcome Collection; and 1910. 4–20. 350).

woven for local consumption and another, quite different, for trade with other peoples. In the sixteenth century cloths woven in Benin were purchased by Europeans for trade in the Gold Coast. At a later period, Yoruba cloths were purchased for trade in Brazil. Cloths have also been woven specifically for use as currency, as in Zaire; and in Sierra Leone at one time cloths of a particular size could be used for paying court fines.

What is a textile?

This is, perhaps, the point at which to define our terms: words such as 'fabric', 'cloth' and 'textile' have been loosely used as if they are interchangeable. The standard work of reference relevant here is Irene Emery's *The Primary Structures of Fabrics* published in 1966 by the Textile Museum, Washington D.C., and the next few paragraphs are very largely drawn from it.

The terms 'fabric' and 'textile' can be distinguished according to their literal meanings and Latin derivations: fabric, from *fabricare*, to make, to build, to 'fabricate', is the generic term for all fibrous constructions; while textile, from *texere*, to weave, refers specifically to woven fabrics. Fabric structures made directly from fibres by simply pressing and matting them into coherence, i.e. felted materials such as barkcloth, must not be confused with fabric structures made by an ordered *interworking* of previously prepared *elements* (the component parts of an interworked fabric). We must also distinguish two systems of interworking: first, the interworking of a single element or set of elements with itself by means of looping, knitting,

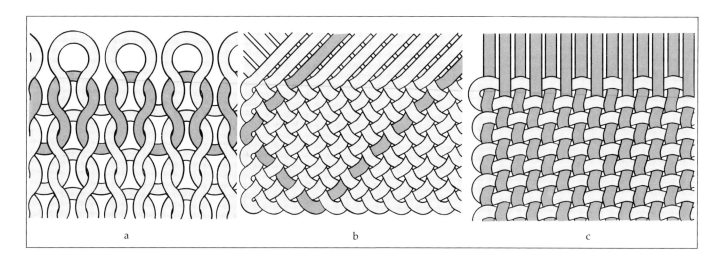

a | b | c

a Looping or knitting, the interworking of a single element with itself, a technique often used in Africa in the manufacture of masquerade costumes.

b The oblique interlacing of a single set of elements, a technique often used in mat-making, called braiding by some and plaiting by others.

c Weaving the interlacing of two sets of elements at right angles to each other.

knotting, netting, braiding, plaiting, etc.; and secondly, the interworking of one set of parallel elements by another set crossing them more or less at right angles. These two sets are essential to the structure of a woven fabric, or textile; and it is, of course, with the woven fabrics of Africa that we are here concerned.

Cloth, a term which is in everyday use, is rather more difficult to define. All textiles are cloths, but not all cloths are textiles, for they need not be woven; and all cloths are fabrics, but, again, not all fabrics are cloths. Thus, to give the obvious example, *basketry* depends on the ordered interworking of previously prepared elements and it is usual to assume a distinction between cloth and basketry. But, as Emery shows in a lengthy discussion, although both words are widely used as generic terms for large groups of fabrics, they are 'variable composites'. The most that can be said is that basketry generally comprises fabrics which, due to the inherent inflexibility of some or all of their components, have little or no pliability; whereas cloth is composed of no inherently inflexible or rigid elements. In other words there is no hard and fast distinction between cloth and basketry (or, for that matter, between either of them and 'matting', a term which has only aggravated the confusion: some of the looms described here, for example, have been described as mat looms despite the fact that their products are worn around the body rather than trodden under foot).

Weaving is, therefore, the technique of interworking two sets of elements; and although it can be effected simply by manipulating the two sets with one's fingers it is made easier if one set can be stretched out in some way. This, at its simplest, is what a loom does; and the set of elements thus held in tension is called the *warp*. The set which is then interlaced with the warp is called the *weft*.

Interlacing is the most straightforward kind of interworking as each element simply passes under or over the elements that cross its path. Each weft element may simply pass under and then over each successive warp element, and the textile is held together simply by reversing the order of passing under and over for each successive weft element.

However, compared with some kinds of knotted and knitted fabrics, the uncomplicated nature of the relationship between warp and weft makes the interlacing process easily adaptable to mechanisation. It is possible to separate the warp elements into two groups, those which lie over and those which lie under a passage of the weft, and, after passing the weft through the opening between these two groups, either reversing or otherwise altering the grouping of the warps for the next passage, or *pick*, of the weft. This opening between the two groups of warp elements is called a *shed* and the device for making it, a *shedding device*. The reversal of the shed for the next pick of the weft is usually called the *countershed*. In addition to giving tension to the warp elements, most looms, therefore, also provide some kind of simple machinery which effects a simultaneous separation of the two groups of warp elements and the reversal of their position after each pick of the weft.

Textile design

We aim to provide a comprehensive view of the ways and means of textile manufacture and design in Africa; and, in so doing, something of the economic, social and other roles played by textiles will inevitably emerge. However, technology rather than function is the principal concern; and textile design depends upon three variable factors: the nature and colour of the fibres employed, the kinds of relationship between warp and weft which may be effected on a loom, and the possible methods of embellishment of a fabric after manufacture. The weaving of any textile presupposes the existence of previously prepared elements. Loose fibres, or fibrous materials, must be transformed into these elements, which are in turn interworked to form the fabric. Therefore the preparation of the raw materials used in textile manufacture is discussed first, followed by an account of the kinds of loom found in Africa and the different ways of giving tension to the warp and of effecting the shed and countershed. This leads to the kind of design which can be achieved by means of relatively simple variations in the basic relationship of warp and weft, made possible by different kinds of shedding device. Finally, the decorative techniques sometimes applied to cloth subsequent to its weaving – dyeing, appliqué, embroidery, quilting, patchwork, drawing, stencilling and printing – are considered.

Male and female weavers

In some areas, for example, most of West Africa, Ethiopia, East Africa and Zaire, all weaving is done by men. Elsewhere, for example Berber North Africa and Madagascar, all the weaving is done by women. In other areas, such as Nigeria, Arab North

A man weaving raphia cloth in the Ndundu region of Zaire. The upright, rectangular structure of his loom is, in principle, very similar to the Nigerian woman's loom in the next illustration.

CHAPTER TWO

THE RAW MATERIALS

A woman of the Ayt Brahim tribe spinning warp yarn. The wool is mounted on a long distaff. The Ayt Brahim are a branch of the Ayt Hadiddu.

The fibres employed in the manufacture of cloth in Africa are bark, bast, cotton, raphia, silk and wool. Bark is felted and the fabric which results is therefore not a textile but in some areas it fills an analogous role while in others it seems to be the precursor of woven cloth. Bast fibres are obtained by retting the stems of certain dicotyledonous plants. Raphia is simply peeled from the leaves of the raphia palm. Wool and cotton, despite their different sources of origin, both undergo a similar range of processes in order to prepare them for spinning, which transforms the raw fibres into *yarn* (the general term for any assemblage of fibres made into a continuous strand suitable for weaving). Wild silk is also spun. Machine-spun cotton, silk, rayon, and nowadays lurex, are also used and in many areas have almost completely replaced the locally made yarns.

Leather, hide and sinew may also be used as alternatives to textiles and in appliqué work but although they are shredded to permit plaiting or braiding, they are not woven. Metals such as gold and silver, and occasionally lead, have been used to embellish a woven cloth either as wire, usually wrapped round a core of some other substance, or in the form of plates, discs, beads and other shapes, particularly in Nigeria, North-east Africa and Madagascar.

Wool

In the African continent wool is harvested principally from sheep, and, to a lesser extent, hair from goats and occasionally from camels, in North Africa, the Sudan and in the area of West Africa immediately south of the Sahara, known as the inland delta of the River Niger or the Niger Bend. The economy of many Berber tribes of Morocco and Algeria is based partly upon sheep rearing, and wool is the most important fibre used in weaving cloth. In the Sudan textiles are made of both wool and cotton, though each on a different loom, by different weavers and for different purposes. In Mali, Fulani weavers of the inland Niger delta weave both cotton and wool on the same type of loom though with structural modifications due to the greater friction of wool fibres and, therefore, the need to facilitate the formation of the shed and countershed. In West Africa woolly sheep are found only in isolated areas such as the inland Niger delta and the Songhai region further downstream. Otherwise the breeds of sheep found in West Africa do not yield a fibre suitable for weaving. Some Tuareg tribes of the Sahara spin the hair of goats and camels for use as cordage and in simple weaving. Both goats' and sheep's wool are used by weavers in the southern parts of Madagascar. There is no indication in the early literature that this is a long-standing

23

tradition, and indeed it appears that the preparation of woollen yarn was introduced in this area by French administrators early in the present century. Its subsequent exploitation may be related to the eradication of silk moths by the inadvertent use of insecticides and the threat posed to local traditions of silk weaving.

The account of wool preparation which now follows comes from unpublished field research by Dr James Bynon among the Ayt Hadiddu of the eastern High Atlas region of Morocco. We are particularly grateful to him for permission to make use of this material.

Most Ayt Hadiddu families own sheep and all men are shepherds or, at least, capable of being so. During the winter months their flocks are kept around the

A team of sheep shearers of the Ayt Yazza tribe, eastern High Atlas, Morocco. The Ayt Yazza are another branch of the Ayt Hadiddu.

permanent villages in the valleys of the Atlas Mountains but when spring comes the sheep are moved up to high pastures, with the shepherds and their families living in tents. Sheep shearing is carried out in May by teams of specialist shearers, often men with few or no sheep of their own. It is an event hedged about with ritual as well as the occasion for feasting when the owner of the sheep is obliged to keep open tent and provide lavish hospitality not only for the shearers but for all comers.

The wool of any fleece can be divided into two kinds, the 'harder', longer, straighter fibres which are used for spinning yarn for the warp, and the 'softer', shorter, more crinkly fibres which are used for spinning yarn for the weft. Some fleeces have more of one type than the other though all have some of both. Turning the wool into yarn and the yarn into cloth is the work of women. They will know fairly exactly how much wool of each quality is needed for any particular garment and select the fleeces accordingly. The wool is washed by beating in cold water without the use of any detergent and then covered and kept in the dark for three days during which time it is thought to increase in volume due to its inherent *baraka*, a sacred quality possessed by certain material such as wool and grain.

Wool for the warp is combed using a pair of combs with long iron spikes set in horn mounted on wood. The wool is placed on the teeth of one comb, pulled off by means

Ayt Yazza women washing wool.
The fleeces are broken up, soaked in cold river water and beaten to emulsify the fats in the wool.

of the second, and then drawn off this second comb by hand in lengths of up to three feet. When sufficient wool has been combed each length is broken up into shorter lengths of about nine inches, and one of these is opened out sideways to make a thin sheet of wool fibres. Several of the short lengths are placed on top of this and the whole is then rolled together in such a way as to produce a spindle-shaped sausage of wool. This is now steamed in a steamer of the kind used in preparing the local food, couscous.

The fibres are now ready for spinning, the process of drawing out and twisting together a mass of relatively short fibres to produce a continuous strand. A distaff and spindle are used; the distaff is essentially a stick on which the prepared fibres are mounted and from which they are drawn. Some Berber tribes use a short distaff held in the left hand; others, including the Ayt Hadiddu, use a longer distaff tucked in the belt leaving both hands free for the spinning process. The spindle is a relatively short slender piece of wood pointed at the upper end and with a whorl mounted at the lower end which acts as a fly-wheel retaining the energy generated by the act of spinning so that the spindle continues to turn and so twist the fibres drawn from the distaff.

Where the long distaff is used a short length of fibres is first drawn down, twisted by

Above Three young women of the Ayt Yazza tribe in a tent at sheep-shearing time. The woman on the left is spinning coarse yarn to make cords with which to tie up the legs of the sheep for shearing. The woman on the right is carding wool prior to the spinning of weft yarn.

Opposite A woman of the Ayt Abderraziq tribe combing wool prior to the spinning of warp yarn. The Ayt Abderraziq are another branch of the Ayt Hadiddu.

hand and attached to the upper tip of the spindle. With the finger and thumb of her right hand the spinner then spins the spindle and with the finger and thumb of her left hand she draws down an appropriate length of fibres. She then slides the finger and thumb of her left hand back up the drawn-out length of fibres thereby permitting the twist induced by the spinning of the spindle to follow them up. The drawing out and spinning continues until the spindle, which hangs spinning freely in mid air, almost touches the ground. The length of yarn so manufactured is then carefully wound onto the spindle to prevent it untwisting, looped around the lower end below the whorl to stop the yarn unwinding, and then brought up and hitched to the upper tip of the spindle to permit the spinning of a further length of yarn. The long distaff tucked in the belt enables the spinner to use both hands in drawing out, spinning and controlling the twisting of the fibres. Where the short distaff is used, however, it is held in the left hand leaving the spinner with only her right hand to perform the three actions which comprise the spinning process.

Preparing the yarn for the weft is a much different process. The shorter, softer fibres are used; they are carded rather than combed, and spun on a much longer spindle in a quite different way and without using a distaff. A pair of cards is used, each consisting of a wooden bat (rather like a square ping-pong bat) with short hook-like wire spikes set in a leather pad mounted on it. Some wool is spread on one card and the other is pulled across it with the angle of the teeth of each card in the opposite direction. By scraping the wool from one to the other two thin sheets of fibres eventually result, one

An unmarried girl of the Ayt Abderraziq carding wool prior to the spinning of weft yarn.

on each card. These are removed and each is split down the middle, and the two halves are joined together to form a ribbon of fibres. To spin them into weft yarn one corner is caught onto the spindle, drawn out and simply wound on. The lower end of the spindle rests on the ground and it is held at an angle towards the spinner so that the fibres wind their way continuously up to the point and slip off. This automatically induces a twist in the fibres and the action is repeated until the twist is sufficient. The length of yarn so produced is finally wound onto the spindle and the process is repeated with another length of drawn-out fibres. The yarn produced by this method has very little strength of itself, unlike the warp yarn which has to withstand great tension when mounted on the loom. As the textiles woven by Berber women are weft-faced (see below) the warp is entirely hidden from view and only weft yarn is therefore dyed for weaving. The materials and processes are described below in the section dealing with indigo and other dyes.

Silk

Silk is the filament secreted by the caterpillar of certain species of moth in the manufacture of their cocoons prior to metamorphosis. Its use in textile manufacture in Africa is more restricted than that of wool, cotton or raphia. In Nigeria wild silk is obtained from the cocoons of various species of moth of the genus *Anaphe*, which breeds on the tamarind tree. The caterpillars are communal by nature and an entire colony, which may comprise several hundred individuals, will spin itself into one large cocoon. The outer layer enclosing the entire assemblage of metamorphosing pupae is light brown in colour, while the inner layers, enclosing each individual, are nearly white. *Anaphe* moths are not domesticated although in parts of northern Nigeria their breeding is encouraged by the cultivation of the tamarind. Collection of the silk nevertheless depends upon chance. If a hunter or a farmer happens to find a cocoon he will take it to the nearest market and sell it. If the cocoon still contains caterpillars he will be able to get a little more for it than if pupation has occurred (in which case the

A young woman of the Ayt Yazza spinning weft yarn.

pupae rattle if the cocoon is shaken), because, when the cocoon is opened, the caterpillars can be roasted and eaten.

In order to use the silk, the gum which binds the filaments of the outer layer of the cocoon must be removed. Wood ash balls (the preparation of which is described below as part of the indigo dyeing process), because of their alkaline content, are stirred into hot water. The cocoon is then broken up and boiled overnight in the ash water to remove the gum. The de-gummed silk is washed clean with several changes of water and dried in the sun; and the mass of silk fibres is now ready to be spun. The spinning process is more or less as described for woollen warp yarn above. The yarn which results has a pale greyish-brown colour, is somewhat coarse in texture, and does not have the sheen typical of silk produced from other species of moth. It is woven by Yoruba and Nupe weavers with a cotton weft, and also used by Nupe and Hausa embroiderers. Garments incorporating wild silk are luxury and prestige items and Yoruba weavers even weave a beige-coloured cotton imitation of wild silk yarn. Its use is now declining, however, as it is being increasingly replaced by factory-made equivalents.

The life-style of the *Anaphe* moth contrasts with that of the cultivated silk moth of Asia and Europe, *Bombyx mori*, whose caterpillars are solitary by nature making it possible to unwind the silk filaments from their individual cocoons. The domesticated silk moth is not found in Africa, except possibly in Madagascar, although its products are. European silk cloths have been unravelled by the Asante of Ghana probably since the seventeenth century in order to incorporate the yarn thus obtained into their own textiles. In the nineteenth century waste silk from Italy and France, magenta in colour, was a significant item of trans-Saharan trade to Kano. In 1897, £6,716 worth of this fibre was included in the Tripoli-Kano caravan (Marion Johnson, 1976). Waste silk was spun in the same way as wool, wild silk or cotton. In the present century imported silk yarn, now completely replaced by rayon, has been widely used by weavers in Ghana and Nigeria. Imported silk cloths have also been employed as cloth, rather than for the

Right An Ebira woman bowing cotton. The bowstring is flicked against the cotton to fluff it out prior to spinning. Nigeria.

Above An Akoko-Edo woman removing the seeds from raw cotton. The iron rod is rolled over the cotton bolls to squeeze out the seeds. Nigeria.

yarn which could be unravelled from them, for example, in the manufacture of Ethiopian ecclesiastical vestments.

Silk is also produced in Madagascar. There are a number of different varieties (up to twenty counted by Linton in the 1920s) of which the native version is *Borocera madagascariensis* which gives a brownish silk. In the nineteenth century, however, *Bombyx mori* was introduced giving a finer, white filament. The former feeds principally on the *tapia* tree and the latter on introduced mulberry. Finally, the island of Pate near Lamu off the Kenya coast appears to have been a centre of silk weaving although the origin of the yarn employed is uncertain.

Cotton

Cotton yarn is spun from the mass of fibres (the boll) surrounding the seeds of the cotton plant, of which there are several species of the genus *Gossypium*. Little is certain about the cultivation or use of cotton in Africa until the eleventh century AD by which time it must have been extensive, at least in West Africa. Large quantities of cotton (and woollen) textiles of a great variety of patterns, indicating the existence of a well-developed textile industry remarkably similar to the present day, have been discovered in the course of the excavations of archaeological deposits of this period in

Akoko-Edo women, Nigeria, spinning cotton. The woman on the left is about to spin her spindle. The woman on the right draws down a further length of fibres while the spindle spins.

the caves of the Bandiagara escarpment of Mali, now the area inhabited by the Dogon people. A full account of this discovery and its implications is given by Venice Lamb (1975). West Africa has without doubt been one of the major world centres of cotton cultivation. (It is unfortunate that so much effort was made by the colonial powers to subvert local cultivation, an effort which for one reason or another has now largely succeeded.) Cotton was also cultivated and woven in the Sudan (cotton fabrics are known from early fifth-century Meroe), Ethiopia and Somalia, and southwards through East Africa to the south of Zimbabwe, as well as in Madagascar where it was introduced by early European visitors.

The first stage in transforming the cotton bolls harvested from the plants into yarn suitable for weaving is ginning, the removal of the cotton seeds. A few bolls are placed on a block of wood, or in some areas on a flat stone, and their seeds are squeezed out by rolling an iron, or sometimes a wooden rod over them. The fibres must then be untangled. This can be done simply by loosening the bolls by hand, although bowing is the usual method. The string of a small bow is plucked against the cotton, hitting it and fluffing it out into a large loose mass.

The technique of spinning cotton fibres, once they are sufficiently loosened, is virtually the same as that used by Berber women to spin their woollen warp yarn

31

(described above). The same three movements can be observed and the spindle spins either freely in midair or in a dish. The cotton is held in the left hand and may or may not be supported by a distaff. With her right hand the spinner spins, draws down and controls the twisting. She may have a small pot of fine ashes in which she periodically dips the finger and thumb of her right hand to prevent them sticking to the cotton fibres.

Cotton fibres grow naturally in more than one colour. White is usual but a pale brown is also common. Brown can also be obtained from several vegetable dyes as can many other colours, to be described below. In Ghana the difficulties of producing a good red dye, however, led to the unravelling of imported red cotton cloths by Asante and Ewe weavers (Johnson, 1978), and in parts of Nigeria red hospital blankets have been unravelled in order to re-weave the yarn thus obtained. At the present time factory-spun and dyed cotton yarns, as well as rayon and lurex, in a wide range of bright colours have largely supplanted the hand-spun cotton except where it is significant in a ceremonial or prestige context. Factory-woven cotton shirting is also widely used both for the manufacture of garments according to local patterns and by Senegalese and Yoruba dyers for indigo resist-dyeing.

Imported cottons have supplanted many of the woollen garments in North Africa. Originally very costly, so that only the rich could afford to buy it, cotton clothing is now cheaper than hand-spun wool and husbands are only too glad to buy such things for their wives, by whom they are still regarded as luxury goods despite the fact that they provide inefficient insulation against the Moroccan winter.

Bast

Bast fibres are the stem structure of dicotyledonous plants such as jute and flax, which are obtained by a process called retting. The stalks are immersed in water for several days to allow bacterial decomposition to detach the bast fibres from the woody core.

In West Africa a very large number of plant species, particularly of the genus *Hibiscus*, yield bast fibres used for netting and cordage. Two species which give fibres fine enough to be spun for use in weaving cloth are *Urena lobata* and *Sida rhombifolia*. The earliest evidence for the use of bast fibres in West Africa is provided by fragments of cloth excavated by Professor Thurstan Shaw at Igbo-Ukwu in Nigeria, a site dated by radiocarbon to the ninth century AD. (Whether cotton was already in use in this area at that time is, of course, not known.) At the present time the use of bast fibres is the exception rather than the rule and when they do occur they are generally woven with cotton. Women of the Yoruba-speaking Owe people of Kabba seem to be the specialists in preparing and weaving this fibre (Boser-Sarivaxévanis, 1975). The cloth they manufacture with it is intended for local ritual use but is in demand as far south as the Benin Kingdom; the Ebira, their immediate southerly neighbours, incorporate bast fibres into one of their more costly types of burial cloth.

In Madagascar, bast fibres are obtained from three different species of tree according to Ralph Linton (1933). All the Malagasy peoples use it for cordage, but its use for cloth is now limited to the peoples to the east of the central plateau, the Tanala, the Zafimaniry and in the past some of the Betsileo. Trees two to three inches in diameter are cut into four-foot lengths and the hard outer bark scraped away. The inner bark is then split lengthwise and taken off in a single sheet. (This is done by men.) The sheets of bark are taken to the village, where the women split them into strips about half an inch wide. The bark is then boiled in water with wood ash for about two hours and the mixture left standing for a day. It is then washed in running water and, while still wet, is picked into fibres suitable for yarn. The fibres are then washed again and kneaded on stone with the feet. They are wrung out and dried for a day in the house, never in the sun. To prepare the yarn a woman sits with a bundle of fibres hung beside her. She draws down the fibres one by one and rolls them between her palm and her thigh, knotting on new fibres as needed. The finished thread is wound around two sticks set in the ground about two feet apart. When sufficient yarn has been prepared in this way to make a skein it is removed from the sticks and put aside ready for the weaving to begin.

A man peeling off the outer layers of the raphia palm leaflet, Anang-Ibibio, south-eastern Nigeria.

Raphia

Early reports from many parts of Africa make reference to the existence of a 'grass' costume and to the weaving of 'grass' fibres. This, however, is a confusion for the grass-like fibre was undoubtedly produced from the raphia palm, which was and remains an important focus of life and economy in many parts of sub-Saharan Africa. It is the source of cordage used in making ropes, fishing tackle and snares; its pulp makes an effective fish poison; it can be tapped to obtain palm wine; the palm midribs serve as roofing poles, stools, loom beams and, more recently, bedsteads; and the raphia leaf provides the fibres from which raphia cloth is woven.

In Africa seven varieties of raphia palm are found. The largest of these can grow to heights in excess of thirty feet and they produce enormous curving pinnate leaves which when measured flat can be up to fifty feet in length, making them the longest leaves of any plant. Their natural habitat is the marsh or swamp, and they thus grow extensively in and on the fringes of the tropical forests of West and Central Africa, and on the island of Madagascar. Some specimens also occur along isolated watercourses in parts of East and South-east Africa.

The practice of extracting a fibre from the younger leaflets of the raphia palm is known in most of these areas and the weaving and plaiting of this fibre has a distribution which is roughly that of the palm itself. Since the introduction of European-made cotton cloths the production of raphia cloth has certainly decreased. It was, however, 'traditional' in many parts of West Africa, throughout the Zaire Basin (taking this to include the fringe regions of Gabon and Angola) and on Madagascar. In all these places the method of extracting the fibre is, or was, more or less the same. Only the younger leaflets are used. Until they are about four to six feet in length these are found folded longitudinally along a strong midrib in such a way that the surfaces

33

Among the Anang-Ibibio in south-eastern Nigeria the raphia lengths are tied together end to end to produce a continuous warp for weaving on the vertical loom of the area.

in contact are those which will ultimately form the upper surfaces of the expanded leaf. The fibre itself is produced from the upper epidermis of the leaflet. To harvest this, the leaflets are first cut from the tree and placed in the shade until a sufficient quantity has been collected. Whilst they are still fresh a small transverse incision is made underneath with a knife close to the base or the tip of the leaflets. This is sufficient to penetrate the softer layers but does not sever the upper epidermis which is protected by more resistant thick-walled cells. The softer tissues may then be easily peeled off either by hand or by turning the knife at an acute angle and pulling the leaflet quickly across its blade leaving behind the upper epidermis. In Madagascar, and in most parts of the Zaire Basin, the leaflet is divided along its midrib and each half is stripped back separately. In West Africa, on the other hand, the practice would seem to have been to treat the whole leaflet at once. As further division of the epidermis is needed in any case before the fibre is ready for weaving it makes no difference to the finished product which of the methods is used.

The freshly-removed epidermis is a translucent membrane which only acquires its familiar yellowish grass-like quality on being dried out. For this operation ten or more membranes are normally tied together in a single hank and placed in the sun. Care is taken to avoid them drying too quickly for if this occurs they tend to twist upon themselves rather like string. They are, therefore, never laid out flat on the ground but

34

are bundled together and turned from time to time. This process takes about half a day after which the hanks have achieved the form known to gardeners and others who use the 'raffia' which was exported in large quantities from Africa.

To prepare the raphia fibres for weaving, however, these dried membranes are divided lengthwise. This is normally done by splitting them with the fingers. In some parts of the Zaire Basin, however, the use of a comb to perform this task has been reported and examples of these combs are to be found in museum collections. The combs themselves are made from palm midribs and have very fine teeth capable of producing the fibres as required by the weaver. Snail shells have also been used in one or two places, the outer edge of the shell being run lengthwise down the membranes as one would with the fingers.

The raphia fibre is now virtually ready to be mounted on the loom and only in Madagascar is any further preparation undertaken. Here a method of twisting the fibre is employed. The practice is to boil the raphia in an alkaline medium, probably a mixture of wood ash and water as in the preparation of wild silk and also of indigo, and then to twist the ends of the individual lengths together to form a longer continuous length. Elsewhere in Africa the twisting of raphia fibre is unknown, and this of course means that unless two or more fibre lengths are tied together at their ends the maximum dimensions of any given warp or weft element, and hence of the resulting cloth, can be no greater than the length of the membrane from which it is prepared. In south-east Nigeria individual fibre lengths are sometimes knotted together to form a continuous length which is then woven in exactly the same way as cotton yarn elsewhere in that country. In the Zaire Basin area raphia was the only fibre woven in the recent past, and the loom in use employed warp and weft elements exactly as derived from the raphia leaflet. As a result the maximum dimension of any given cloth was about three to four feet square, i.e. the average length of the raphia foliole. When larger cloths were required smaller ones were simply sewn together.

Indigo and other dyes

Wool and cotton yarn, raphia and, in Madagascar, bast fibres are frequently dyed before they are woven; and by far the most extensively used non-industrial dye in Africa is indigo. It is obtained from several plants of the genus *Indigofera*, which are both wild and cultivated, and from *Lonchocarpus cyanescens*, the indigo vine or Yoruba wild indigo which is regarded by Yoruba dyers as giving the more permanent dye. All these plants contain indican, a sugar and indigo compound, fermentation of which releases indoxyl and this, on exposure to air, becomes a mixture of indigo-red and indigo-blue. The first colour is obtained by slow oxidation in an acid medium, the second by rapid oxidation in an alkaline medium. The preparation of the dye therefore has two parts: breaking up the plant structure to facilitate the fermentation process; and preparing the alkaline medium, which, in addition to encouraging the release of indigo-blue, also acts as a mordant serving to fix the dye colour in the yarn or cloth, as the case may be. Details of the preparation process naturally vary from place to place. The description given below is a Yoruba method as described by Nancy Stanfield (1971).

Fresh green leaves of whichever indigo plant is available (it happens to be *Lonchocarpus* in this particular case) are pounded in a mortar and the pulp moulded into balls. These are allowed to dry in the sun for two or three days during which time fermentation begins.

Preparation of potash for the alkaline medium is more complicated. The basic apparatus is a kiln built of mud about four feet high and four feet wide. The top of the kiln is open and about a foot below the top, across the inside, is a perforated mud shelf. At ground level there is a hole in the side through which the kiln is fired. Dry wood is collected for the firing. Short lengths of very green wood are cut and laid across the perforated shelf up to the top of the kiln. Wood ash is moulded into balls with water from a dye pot in which the dye itself has been exhausted; and these balls are piled up on top of the green wood. The kiln is then fired for ten to twelve hours

A comb used among the Kuba, Zaire, for splitting raphia fibres. Length 4 in (10 cm). 1910. 4–20. 99.

Yoruba women pounding indigo leaves. The pulp is moulded into balls which are then dried in the sun.

and left to cool until the third day. The ashes of the green sticks, the ash balls which covered them and which are now broken up, and ash from the dry wood that fired the kiln, are moulded into balls, again using exhausted dye water, and allowed to dry in the sun. The best quality ash is, of course, that obtained from the green sticks and it is not mixed with the other. Ash balls and indigo balls surplus to the dyer's own needs can be sold in the market.

The alkaline medium for the rapid oxidation of indoxyl is prepared using two large pots. One, which is dug into the ground to stop it falling over, has a hole in its side. The other is stood upon the first and has a hole in the bottom. This hole is covered with a sieve made from small sticks and discarded indigo plant fibres from the dye pots. Some of the ash balls are broken, mixed with ash from the cooking fire, and placed upon the sieve. Water is added, which drips through to the pot below taking the potash with it. As the water filters through it is scooped out via the hole in the side and transferred to a dye pot. When it has all filtered through the ash is removed and replaced, and filtering begins again. This procedure continues until enough ash water is obtained. Ash which has been used in this way will either be kept and moulded into balls, together with ash from the cooking fire, to be re-fired in the kiln or it is discarded in a heap at the back of the dyer's house.

Dyeing is always carried out in the shade and the dye pots, which are also dug into the earth to prevent them falling over, are kept covered. The number of indigo balls to be used depends on the strength of colour desired. Fifty balls produce a good blue and a hundred and fifty a really intense colour. The indigo balls are broken up and placed in a dye pot, and ash water is poured over them until the pot is full. The contents of the pot will be stirred from time to time during the next three days and then dyeing commences. The dye itself, it will be noticed, is cold.

The yarn or cloth which is to be dyed is immersed for two minutes or so and then

36

Firing a wood-ash kiln, Yoruba, Nigeria.

lifted out, dripping, onto a board which drains back into the dye pot. It will be dipped like this three or four times and then put to dry in the sun. This will be repeated until the desired colour is produced. For the best quality of colour, fresh dye will be used for each series of dippings. The objects dyed are always allowed to drip dry and are never wrung out. When first removed from the dye pot the colour of the article is green but this soon deepens to blue. As the liquid in the pot is soaked up, it is topped up with ash water. Eventually all the dye is absorbed and the water which remains is used for moulding the ash balls. In any case, the dye only keeps for five days.

Cloth which has been dyed is finished by beating with wooden mallets over a piece of tree trunk or some other rounded wooden object. As the cloth is invariably overloaded with dye the beating produces a metallic sheen. This will be lost as soon as it is washed.

The basis of the indigo-dyeing process is constant because of the chemical properties of the various substances involved in it, although there is more than one way, even within Yorubaland, of inducing fermentation and of preparing the alkaline medium (sometimes called a 'lye'). The economic basis also seems to be constant for indigo-dyeing and is almost everywhere a specialist activity, unlike dyeing in other colours. The indigo-dyers in a community, certainly in West Africa, are usually women, as among the Yoruba, although in some areas, such as Hausaland, the indigo-dyers are men. The Hausa city of Kano was famous for its dye pits in the mid-nineteenth century when it was estimated that it had some two thousand of them. (Instead of dye pots the Hausa dig large pits in the ground and line them with a local cement as used in building.) Elsewhere in West Africa, peoples particularly famous for their indigo-dyeing are the Baule of the Ivory Coast and the Soninke or Sarakole of Senegal.

As we are here concerned with raw materials and the preparation of yarn prior to weaving, although the technique of indigo-dyeing is the same whether yarn or woven cloth is the subject of attention, consideration of the various methods of resist-dyeing woven textiles is left until later. This is, however, the appropriate point to mention the technique of resist-dyeing yarn before it is woven, a technique known as 'ikat'. Several lengths of yarn are tied together at intervals before being immersed in the indigo. Where the yarn is tied the dye is, of course, resisted so that lengths of yarn are produced which change colour at intervals. Weavers of the Hausa, Yoruba and Northern Edo peoples, as well as the Ewe of Ghana, employ 'ikat'-dyed yarn in some of their patterns of warp stripes. The Baule produce relatively complex patterns by this method according to the alignment of the tied areas in the warp. The most elaborate

Dipping cloth into the dye pot, Yoruba, Nigeria. Skeins of yarn dyed a pale blue are to be seen beside the dyer.

use of the 'ikat' technique, however, occurred amongst some Sakalava groups in Western Madagascar.

Indigo gives various shades of colour from the palest blue to a deep, intense 'black', but African weavers are not limited to this range of colours. Among the Berbers of Morocco, weft yarn may be dyed red, black, yellow, blue and green, using locally-available vegetable dyes. Red is obtained by boiling yarn with the dried and pounded root of the madder plant together with the juice of a bitter variety of pomegranate, which is the mordant. There are three sources of the colour black: naturally black wool; pomegranate skin, or evergreen oak bark, either of which dye the yarn yellow and this is turned black ('saddened') with iron sulphate purchased in local markets; and indigo, which also provides blue. The root of another plant gives yellow and a second dyeing with indigo gives green. Brilliant white is also sometimes used against the natural wool with cotton. As elsewhere indigo-dyeing is a specialist craft whereas the other dye colours are applied by the spinners and weavers themselves.

In West Africa many shades of red, yellow, blue, green, brown and black are available from local vegetable and mineral sources. Imperato (1973) gives an account of the dyes used by the Fulani of the inland Niger delta region of Mali. To dye yarn black it is first boiled with the leaves of two trees, *Anogeissus* and *Combretum*, which turns it yellow. The yarn is then totally immersed for several days in a pot containing mud, which turns it black. Yellow can be obtained using the first half of the method just described but a more stable colour is produced by boiling the yarn with sheep's dung and a wild mushroom which has been dried and powdered. The best red is obtained by boiling already yellow yarn with the flowers of *Hibiscus cannabinus*, the hemp-leaved hibiscus (the stem of which yields a bast fibre widely used for cordage).

It would be impossible to list all the sources of dyes used in West Africa in addition to indigo. However, here is a selection: turmeric, kola nuts and a yellow flowering plant, *Cochlospermum tinctorium*, give different shades of yellow; a species of guinea corn cultivated only for its dye content, *Sorghum caudatum*, as well as henna and the camwood trees, *Baphia* and *Pterocarpus*, give reds; *Sorghum caudatum* if immersed in forest mud gives a black dye; the bark of various trees such as *Parkia* (the locust bean), *Acacia* and *Anogeissus* gives browns, in addition to the naturally brown cotton; and the colour green can be obtained by dyeing yarn yellow first of all and then with indigo.

For the Kuba of Zaire, Torday and Joyce (1910) give red, yellow, black and white as the usual colour range of Kuba textiles. The red is obtained from camwood, i.e. *Pterocarpus* spp., properly called barwood (*Baphia nitida*, the true camwood tree, does not occur in the Zaire Basin); yellow from the brimstone tree (*Morinda* spp.); black from mud, charcoal or plant sources, and white from kaolin. This does not, however, exhaust the colour range of Zairian textiles. Various plant species give blues, orange and purple, which is quite common among the Ngongo, though not, it seems, among other Kuba sub-groups.

In Madagascar, a black dye is prepared by crushing the leaves of a particular tree and boiling with ferruginous earth; yellow is obtained from turmeric roots; orange is prepared from the roots of one tree and red from the bark of another; and blue is obtained using indigo. In Uganda the black dye used on some Ganda barkcloth is prepared from swamp mud mixed with various vegetable substances.

Barkcloth and other felted fabrics

Finally, we come to barkcloth, a species of cloth which is not a textile in the strictest sense of the word for it is not woven. Nevertheless in those parts of Africa where barkcloth is or was found it performed comparable functions to woven cloth: it was used as clothing, for bedding, as a wall covering, and so forth. Indeed, barkcloth was often produced in areas where weaving was not practised, and there are some indications that where the felting of bark fibre and the production of woven fabrics were both found in one place, the process of felting was in fact the older technique. Amongst the Kuba, for instance, woven raphia cloth provided the clothing for everyday wear and for most ceremonial purposes. Barkcloth, however, was still occasionally produced in historic times and was known amongst the Kuba as the clothing of the ancestors. When it was used in ceremonial or ritual contexts the effect was to provide a physical reference to the past; its use recalled the ancestors, and was therefore highly prized even if, by comparison with the elaborate decoration on raphia cloths, it was visually the less exciting. These considerations suggest that some mention of the distribution, methods of production, and use of barkcloth is relevant in a book nominally devoted to 'textiles'.

The best-known centres of barkcloth production in Africa are in the central part of the continent, in the area of the Zaire Basin, Rwanda, Uganda, Malawi and Zambia. It was also to be found elsewhere. The Asante people of Ghana, for instance, produced a barkcloth which, it is recorded, was widely traded amongst the forest peoples of the Ivory Coast. Nowadays barkcloth production has been completely overshadowed by the weaving of the silk and cotton cloths for which the Asante are famous. Barkcloth is also recorded from Liberia, Togo and south-east Nigeria. In Madagascar barkcloth supplemented cloths woven in silk, cotton, raphia, and wool. However, in many parts

The later stages in removing the bark. The process as illustrated here was observed amongst the Ganda, Uganda.

Barkcloth was the traditional wear of both men and women amongst the Ganda. The man to the right is holding one of the mallets with which he prepares barkcloth.

of Central Africa the only alternative to barkcloth was prepared skin and the manufacture and use of barkcloth was proportionately greater. Amongst the Ganda, for instance, many villages had their own plantations of 'barkcloth' trees amongst the banana and coffee groves and most of the men were competent in producing the cloth and were expected to provide for the needs of their families. Upwards of fifty varieties of barkcloth were recognised by the Ganda alone and special types of cloth were reserved exclusively for courtly use. Nowhere else in Africa was barkcloth production so extensive that it could generate as comprehensive a typology or provide a material expression of the differing status of the individuals within a community.

The tree which is most widely used in the manufacture of barkcloth in Uganda, as elsewhere in Africa, is a species of fig, *Ficus natalensis*. However, cloths of different qualities may be produced by using other species of the same genus. The tree has a characteristically straight trunk and is topped by an umbrella of foliage. It is the lower bark (up to the point where the tree begins to branch out) which is taken to produce the cloth. The bark itself is easily removed. First the outer hard surface is scraped off, usually with a knife; then circular incisions are made at the upper and lower levels of the main trunk and a single vertical incision is run down between the two. A tool made from a sharpened section of banana leaf spine, or in some cases a section of the fruit-bearing stem of the banana, is worked in behind the exposed layer of bark which is carefully peeled away in a single cylindrical strip. The average dimensions for such a strip would be about twelve feet by two feet. This process of stripping the bark does not damage the tree as the whole of the exposed trunk is immediately swathed in a bandage of banana leaves to protect it from exposure to the sun and the wind. After about a week the tree has already regenerated sufficiently for this protective covering to be removed. Any subsequent damage to the newly forming bark may be treated by the application of a poultice of sheep's dung. This process of removing the bark may be repeated as many as thirty or forty times and indeed the qualities of the bark seem to be enhanced by this procedure. Before the bark can be beaten out to give a flexible cloth it must first be moistened to make it soft. This may involve it being completely immersed in water, a practice found for instance in parts of north-eastern Zaire. In Uganda the bark is rolled up in a bundle of banana leaves and steamed over a small fire of green logs. The moisture in the leaves and in the logs themselves is transferred to the stripped bark during the process of cooking it, and this also has the effect of changing the bark from a brownish colour to a rich yellow. In other places the bark is moistened simply by leaving it for several days in a suitably damp and shady place. Whichever method is used, however, the moistened bark is still in a relatively fragile condition when it is ready for beating out. For this reason it is rolled up before being beaten, and gradually unrolled as the work proceeds.

The long task of beating is normally carried out by one man, although for the making of larger cloths, teams of three or even four men may work together. They sit side by side in a special shelter usually furnished only with a narrow tree trunk set horizontally and firmly in the ground, its top surface shaped with an adze to act as a kind of anvil. The beating tools are normally heavy wooden mallets, varying in shape and size although those found in the Zaire Basin area are often carved of ivory. The head of the mallet is grooved or cross-hatched to assist in felting the bark fibre. In Uganda a set of beaters, each with grooves of differing degrees of fineness, is used. Those with the widest and deepest grooves are used first for the main work and the finer ones for the process of finishing off. By this method a very thin cloth is produced but one which, because the fibres are so finely intermeshed, is still relatively resilient.

In the process of beating out the width of the bark strip is increased by upwards of five times, but the length, because the fibres run longitudinally, only by about one-tenth. Thus a piece of bark measuring ten feet by two feet will yield a cloth measuring about eleven feet by ten feet. The wider and finer cloths are those used for clothing, whilst the thicker less flexible cloths are reserved for purposes such as bedding. The final stage in the process is to place the beaten cloth in the sun where, after several days, through a gradual process of oxidation, it acquires a progressively deepening reddish brown colour. Amongst the Asante a type of bark was used which produced a whitish cloth. This was also formerly found in Uganda where the trees producing it were the exclusive property of the royal court. The distinctive colour of most African barkcloth, however, is the rich reddish brown. This was usually left undecorated, but in some parts (again most notably in Uganda) stencilled patterns were applied to the cloth.

The felting of fibres of animal origin, namely wool and human hair, is not unknown in Africa though it seems to be extremely rare. One example is provided by the black woollen cloaks manufactured in the highlands of Ethiopia. Another is the small head-dresses found in parts of Uganda, Kenya, and the southern Sudan, which incorporate sections of felted human hair in their structure.

CHAPTER THREE

THE
LOOM

A weaver seated at her loom, eastern Yoruba, Nigeria. The warp is stretched between two parallel beams. Her feet rest in a pit dug beneath the loom.

There are three basic points to remember about the weaving of a textile. First, there are two sets of elements which interlace with each other at right angles; and it is possible to manufacture cloth simply by manipulating the elements with the fingers, as we have already pointed out. Some Tuareg tribes of the Sahara weave simple bags in this way using a yarn spun from the hair of camels and goats (Nicolaisen, 1963; weaving on a loom is said to be unknown among the Tuareg). Secondly, the interlacing of the two sets is made easier if one of them, called the warp, is held in tension. Thirdly, the interlacing can be made easier still by some mechanical device to separate alternate warp elements into two groups between which pass the elements of the other set, called the weft. The opening between the two groups is called the shed and the mechanism, a shedding device. A loom therefore does two things, it gives tension to the warp and it provides some kind of shedding device.

Methods of applying warp tension

In Africa a widespread method of keeping the warp in tension is to stretch it between two parallel beams. Individual warp elements may be attached to the beams in single lengths, or the warp may be wound around them in a continuous length. Sometimes the warp is applied continuously around posts which are themselves then incorporated into the structure of the loom. The warp is held in tension by holding the beams apart either by pegging them to the ground (in which case it may be known as a 'ground loom'), or by mounting them on a framework, or in some other way. Looms employing this method, with the warp elements mounted in a horizontal plane, are found scattered through almost every part of the continent and were possibly more thoroughly widespread than they now are.

In eastern Africa from Tanzania southwards and in almost all parts of Madagascar this is the only type of loom that occurs. The only region where it does not appear seems to be the Zaire Basin area. Mounted on a framework which is set vertically or at an oblique angle, rather than horizontally, however, this method of warp tension is found in Berber North Africa, Sierra Leone, Nigeria, Cameroun and Zaire, though with significant differences.

The alternative, and more geographically-restricted, means of applying tension to the warp is provided by a framework to which only one end of the warp is attached. The other end is attached either to a weight, as in West Africa, or to a peg driven into the ground, the method found in the Sudan and Ethiopia. On this loom the warp is always mounted more or less horizontally.

Tukulor weavers at Brikama, Gambia. The far end of the warp is attached to a sledge upon which a heavy weight is placed to ensure sufficient tension.

Shedding devices

The simplest shedding device found in Africa is the *shed stick* which is placed between alternate warp elements thus separating them into two groups allowing the weft to be passed through. For the next pick of the weft, however, the relative position of the warp elements must be reversed, if a coherent fabric is to be achieved, so that warp elements formerly to one side of the weft are now on the other, and vice versa. To make this reversal possible, those warp elements which are behind the shed stick (or below, according to the plane in which the loom is mounted) are attached to another stick, called a *heddle*, by means of loops of thread so that they can be pulled forward to form the countershed. The heddle is, of course, placed in front of (or above) the warp, with the loops, or *leashes*, passing between the elements of the one group and around the elements of the other. Once the weft has been passed through, the tension applied by the heddle is released and the warp elements will tend to return to their original position. Shed and countershed are thus effected by alternately manipulating the heddle or the shed stick. On some looms, however, the heddle is fixed and shed and countershed are made simply by manipulating the shed stick. This kind of shedding device, which we shall refer to as a *single-heddle* with shed stick, is consistently associated with the looms employing fixed beams to apply tension to the warp.

The second type of shedding device consists of a pair of heddles. Each in principle operates in the same way as the single-heddle although the construction (to be described in Chapter Five), appearance and method of operation are quite different. Each heddle is joined to the other by a cord which passes over a pulley suspended above the loom, or by some other means; and they are operated by foot pedals.

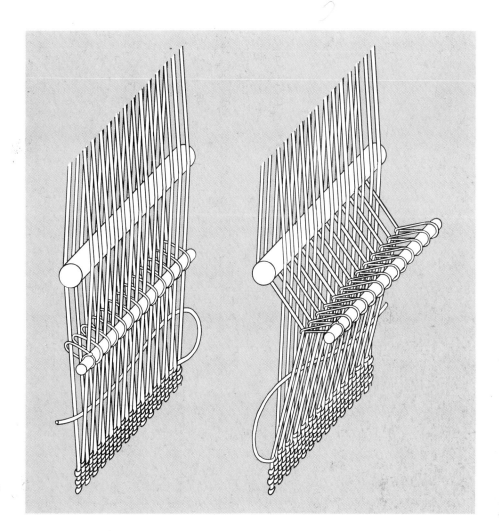

The single-heddle shedding device
showing how shed and countershed are
effected by means of a shed stick, which
separates the warps into their two groups,
and a heddle, leashed to one of these. (The
weaving sword used to beat in the weft is
omitted for the sake of clarity.)

Sakata boy, Zaire, weaving raphia cloth
using a footstrap loom (typologically
related to the first of the two methods of
achieving warp tension described in the
text). The shedding device consists of a
single-heddle, which he holds in his left
hand, together with, above it, a shed stick.

Because of the way the two heddles are connected to each other, depressing one pedal, and therefore the heddle to which it is attached, has the immediate effect of raising the other. Whereas in the case of the single-heddle only one group of warp elements is leashed to a heddle, here both groups are leashed, each to one or other of the pair of heddles. Alternate depression of the pedals thus instantaneously effects the shed and countershed, leaving the weaver's hands free to pass successive picks of the weft to and fro between the warp elements as quickly as the operation of the foot pedals permits. Clearly this mechanism, which we shall refer to as the *double-heddle*, is by far the more efficient and speedy of the two shedding devices. For all that, its distribution is geographically more limited. It is associated with the second of the two methods described above for giving tension to the warp.

A third shedding device consists of a set of perforated cards or 'tablets' through which the warp elements pass. The cards are turned or twisted to effect the shed and countershed. This is the technique known as *tablet weaving* and is found in some parts of North Africa (see, for example, van Baal, 1969) but although it might be expected immediately to the south of the Sahara it has not in fact been reported there. It is, of

A weaver of the Tukulor people at St Louis, Senegal. This loom employs the double-heddle shedding device and in this illustration the shed is open and awaits the passage of the weft. In addition note, in contrast to the Yoruba loom illustrated in Chapter 5, the large pulley and long pedals, the shallow trough (here lined with sacking) dug beneath the loom to make room for the weaver's feet, and the roughly carpentered framework.

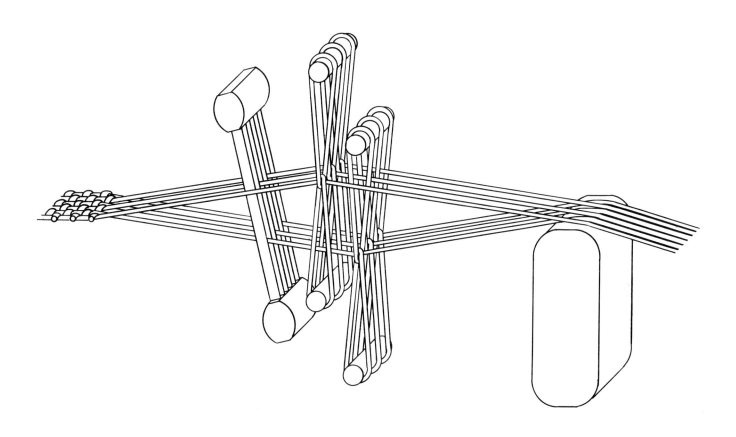

A section through a double-heddle loom. The beater is used to 'beat in' each passage or pick of the weft. Shed and countershed are formed by moving the heddles alternately up and down.

course, widespread throughout other areas of the world and is employed to make narrow bands of cloth. However, it is only of marginal importance to the subject of textile manufacture throughout the African continent and we do not propose to consider it further.

For our present purpose, therefore, all African looms have either a single-heddle or a double-heddle shedding device. This is their one most consistent distinguishing feature and it provides us with the simplest means of classifying them for the purposes of description.

The structural basis of textile design

The design possibilities of the weaving process clearly depend upon the relationship between variations of texture or colour of the yarn employed and the variations of structure which are created according to the different ways in which warp and weft elements can be interlaced with each other. For this reason the following glossary of useful technical terms is relevant to those aspects of textile design in Africa which are functions of the weaving process itself. Here, as before, Irene Emery (1966) is the indispensable guide.

Simple and compound weaves: The basic distinction to be understood at this point is between *simple weaves*, which have only one set each of warp and weft elements, and *compound weaves*, which have more than one set of either warps or wefts or both.

Simple weaves: The simplest possible order of interlacing the weft with the warp is over-one/under-one, and the structure which results is called *plain weave* (also known as 'tabby', 'cloth weave', 'linen weave', etc.). Any other order produces a *float weave*.

Plain weave: The nature of a textile which has an over-one/under-one interlacing structure can be varied by using elements of different thickness, flexibility, or colour, and by spacing the elements of one set further apart than the other. Single elements may also be doubled or tripled or grouped into larger units. (If the units of both warp and weft each have an equal number of elements the structure which results is often called 'basket weave'; if the units of only one set are multiple the structure is called 'half-basket weave'.) Nevertheless, if the order of interlacing is consistently over-one/under-one (and if, of course, there is one set each of warp and weft) the fabric structure is plain weave, whatever differences a woven cloth may present as a result of these variations.

Balanced plain weave: If the elements or units of warp and weft are roughly equal in thickness, flexibility and spacing the structure which results is called *balanced plain weave*. Both warp and weft are equally visible in the completed textile as, for example, in the raphia cloths of Zaire.

Warp-faced plain weave: If, however, the warps are greater in number relative to the number of wefts and are more closely packed together, the warp will dominate and tend to hide the weft. The resulting structure is called *warp-faced plain weave*. The use of warp elements of different colours will produce stripes along the length of the cloth. The cotton and silk cloths of West Africa provide many examples of this. The effectiveness of introducing wefts of different colours into a warp-faced structure will depend upon the degree of predominance of the warp. (The term 'warp-faced' is used in this book in an intentionally loose sense: the totally warp-faced cloth is rare whereas some degree of warp predominance is common.)

Weft-faced plain weave: If, on the other hand, the relative spacing of warps and wefts is reversed so that it is the weft elements which are greater in number relative to the warp elements, and more closely packed together, the weft will dominate and tend to hide the warp, and the structure is called *weft-faced plain weave*. The use of wefts of different colours will produce stripes across the cloth. The introduction of warps of different colours in a weft-faced structure would be visually ineffective. Berber weaving in North Africa is weft-faced. In West Africa some peoples weave both warp-faced and weft-faced fabrics while the Asante of Ghana manage to alternate the two structures in one length of cloth.

Tapestry weave: In a warp-faced textile areas of colour are limited in shape to stripes along the cloth simply because warp colour must be arranged when the warp elements are mounted on the loom. (This would not necessarily apply to compound weaves in which there are two sets of warps, but this kind of complexity is rare if not unknown traditionally in Africa.) This restriction need not apply to a *weft-faced* textile, however, for the simple reason that the very weaving process itself consists of interlacing the weft elements with the warp one pick at a time. Furthermore, although the weft may be worked back and forth across the whole width of the cloth (in which case it is termed 'continuous'), it is equally possible to work a weft of one colour only part of the way across and to finish the row with a weft of another colour. By this method areas of different colours of almost any shape or size (and not restricted to mere stripes) can be built up simply by working each weft back and forth in its own colour areas. Such wefts are termed 'discontinuous' and this variation of weft-faced plain weave is known as *tapestry weave*. It is to be found particularly in Berber North Africa and very occasionally in West Africa.

Weft-inserts: Sometimes small areas of colour may be incorporated into a weft-faced textile by means of *weft inserts*, i.e. by inserting an additional weft and working it back and forth within a small area between two of the main wefts, which, as the weaving continues, will adjust themselves around the inserts.

Plain-weave openwork: A final variation of plain-weave structure is made by weaving the

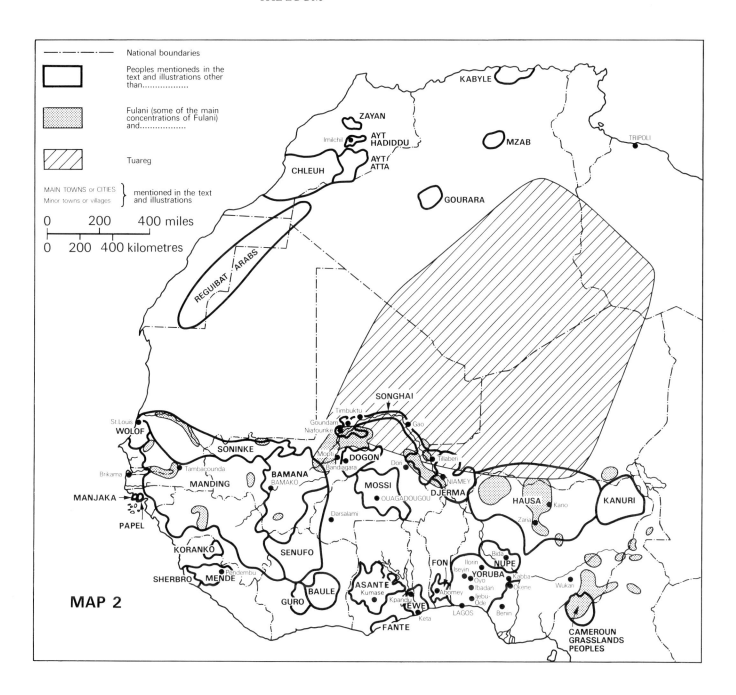

North and West Africa.

weft only part of the way across the cloth and then reversing it one or more times before working it right across again. This produces a gap in the fabric structure, and a series of these gaps is called *openwork* and is an embellishment sometimes used by Hausa and Yoruba weavers in Nigeria. They also imitate plain-weave openwork by inserting the teeth of a comb, or some similar tool, between the warp elements so that the wefts are displaced as they are worked through. However, the openwork effect which this produces will with time look like uneven weaving.

Float weaves: Any numerical order of warp-weft interlacing other than the over-one/ under-one of a simple weave produces a *float weave*. It is obvious that if an element of either warp or weft does not pass under or over one of the opposite set it can only pass, or 'float', under or over more than one; and clearly if a weft element floats over two or more warps on one face of a fabric those warps will be seen to float on the other face. In West Africa small areas or bands of float weave are sometimes introduced as a cotton. In the nineteenth and early twentieth century magenta-coloured European waste silk was spun to give a yarn which enjoyed considerable vogue with Hausa and Yoruba weavers. Raphia and bast fibres are occasionally used in combination with cotton. The ninth-century bast fibre textile fragments discovered at Igbo-Ukwu (Shaw, 1977) are likely to have been woven on a loom of this type, as Renée Boser-Sarivaxévanis (1975) has pointed out.

The vertical single-heddle loom is found among the Yoruba, the various Edo-speaking peoples, the Ebira of the Okene area south-west of the Niger-Benue confluence, the Nupe, the Hausa and possibly other peoples, and in addition there is its occurrence among many Igbo groups, particularly at Akwete, a village in southern Igboland. It is used by women and in the past would have been their principal source of clothing material; for example, in Akoko-Edo (or North-west Edo) two pieces of cloth would be woven and sewn together selvedge to selvedge. (The *selvedge* is the edge of a textile formed as the weft turns back to make the next pick.) A woman will wear such a cloth wrapped around her body and tucked in. If the cloth is for a man, three somewhat narrower pieces are woven and sewn together, and he will wear it either loosely thrown over one shoulder, perhaps when relaxing at home (although elsewhere in West Africa this would be the normal mode of dress), or else cut up and sewn to make a simple shirt and shorts for rough work. A woman's best clothes will be another cloth of the same kind as woven for daily use, perhaps with a distinctive pattern, whereas a man's best clothes will be a wide-sleeved gown made from cloth woven on the double-heddle loom. In areas such as Ebira or Akoko-Edo, where men do not weave, these gowns are imported ready made by local cloth merchants.

With the advent of factory-woven cloths women no longer have to weave for domestic use although they still continue to do so. Where this type of loom now survives it is often because the cloth woven on it has prestige or ritual value, or because it can be sold for cash. Thus, in the late 1960s, Ebira women wove hand-spun cotton according to one particular set of patterns for local use in wrapping up corpses and for masquerade costumes; another set of patterns was provided principally for sale to traders for sale elsewhere in Nigeria for use on deckchairs and as rough clothing for farmers. For domestic use almost the only hand-spun cloth then woven was plain white. They also wove cloths with supplementary weft patterns made with machine-spun cotton or rayon on a machine-spun cotton or rayon ground weave (i.e. cotton on cotton, rayon on cotton, rayon on rayon, but never cotton on rayon). These cloths were mostly purchased by traders for sale to European and well-to-do Nigerian ladies in the major cities of Lagos, Ibadan, Kano, etc. (Akwete cloth, also woven of machine-spun cotton and embellished with supplementary weft float patterns, is similarly disposed of.) In the 1970s lurex became incorporated, usually combined with cotton in the warp.

Immediately south of Ebira, Akoko-Edo women wove hand-spun yarn according to one set of indigo and white warp-stripe patterns for use in wrapping corpses, and according to another set of indigo and white warp-stripe patterns for their own personal use as a prestige cloth worn only on special occasions. Yet another range of indigo and white patterns of stripes, this time also incorporating a red stripe, was made for use by girls at their betrothal ceremonies; and one further kind of hand-spun cotton cloth was woven for sale to Igbo traders. They too also wove in machine-spun cotton and rayon with supplementary weft floats, much of which in the late 1960s found its way to a craft shop in Benin City.

Among the Ebira and the north-west Edo in the late 1960s weaving continued to flourish due to these particular conditions. Every house was found to contain as many looms as there were married women living there. Women's weaving also continues to flourish among the Nupe, at the northern Yoruba town of Ilorin, in eastern Yorubaland (Ekiti, Kabba, etc.), and at Ijebu-Ode in the south. Elsewhere among the Yoruba, in contrast, the single-heddle loom is now hard to find presumably because the kinds of demand which cause Ebira and Akoko-Edo (and Akwete) weaving to flourish are met in central and western Yoruba areas by the products of the man's double-heddle loom.

Pages 78–9 Detail of a cotton and rayon textile, Ebira, Nigeria. Red, yellow and green rayon supplementary wefts on a dark blue cotton ground. The patterns in this example seem to be inspired by similarly-patterned narrow strip cloths woven at Ilorin.

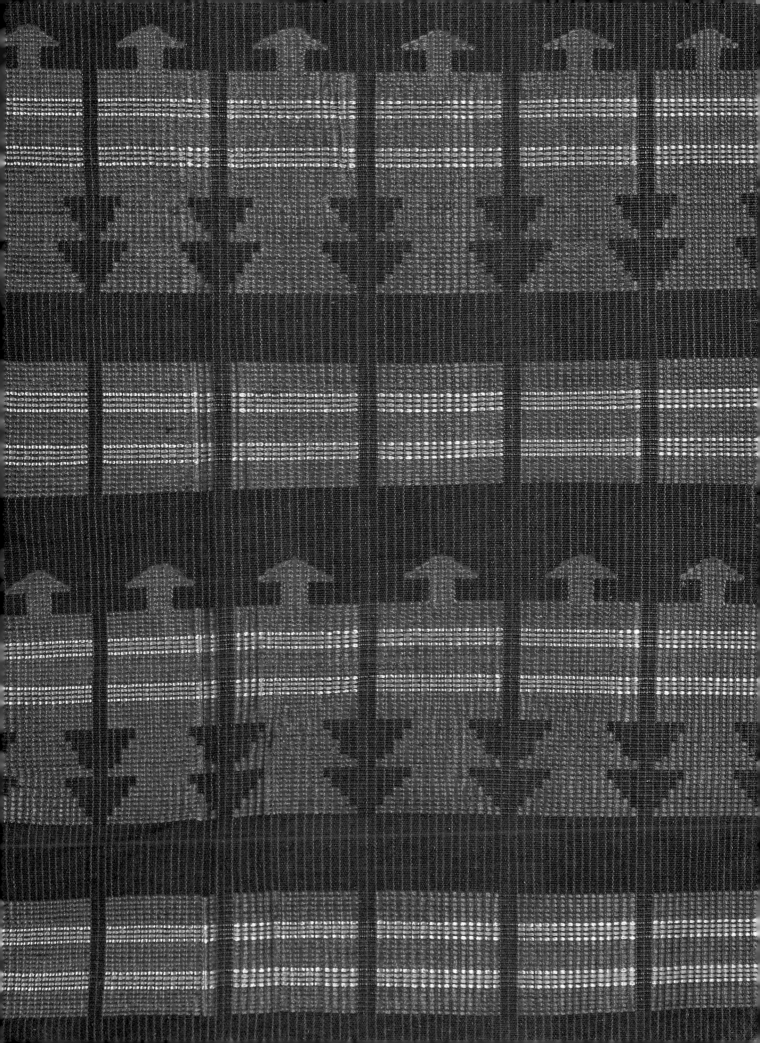

Above Detail of a cotton textile, Nupe, Nigeria. Woven by a woman on the upright single-heddle loom; of red and yellow machine-spun yarn, with supplementary weft patterns, in two pieces each about 20 in (50 cm) wide. 1938. 4–2. 1.

Pages 80–1 Senior members of the Oshugbo secret society at Ijebu-Igbo in southern Yorubaland. The two men seated front left wear cloths woven by the women at Ijebu-Ode and patterned with supplementary weft floats. The man standing back right wears cloth also patterned with supplementary weft floats but in a quite different style and woven by men, possibly at Ilorin in northern Yorubaland. Others are wearing warp-striped cloths woven by Yoruba women.

It may be significant that in none of the above examples is hand-spun cotton used in cloths which have supplementary weft patterning, either for the ground weave or for the extra wefts. This might suggest that the spread of these techniques among most of the women weavers of Nigeria is relatively recent. Among the Ebira the use of supplementary weft floats is almost certainly only around fifty to sixty years old and the various patterns woven in this way seem to be derived from the weaving of other peoples, as we shall see. All the examples of Akwete weaving that we have examined, including those which date back to the late nineteenth century, are also woven entirely of imported machine-spun yarn despite the fact that hand-spun cotton, raphia and bast are said to have been woven there.

Akwete supplementary weft-float patterns are of particular interest in this context not simply because they are frequently elaborate and complex, incorporating tortoises among many other motifs, but especially because they are likely to have developed from the similar though less well-known weaving of the women of Ijebu-Ode in southern Yorubaland. Ijebu-Ode is also the one place where hand-spun yarn has been used to weave cloths embellished with supplementary weft-float patterns. This may indicate the relatively greater antiquity of this style of patterning at Ijebu-Ode in contrast to the other examples of it discussed so far. The precise nature of the link between the two places and of the stimulus to the development of weaving at Akwete has been the subject of field research by Lisa Aronson and her publications (1980a, 1980b, 1982) are recommended as of considerable interest. For various reasons,

Akwete weaving is now so widely known that its patterns are copied by Ebira and other women weavers in Nigeria. As a result it is often impossible to tell from the patterns where exactly a particular cloth was made. Genuine Akwete cloths seem to be the broadest produced on this loom and the very broad web must now be considered their principal distinguishing feature.

Another source of inspiration for supplementary weft patterns, particularly among Ebira weavers, seems to be the decorative weaving of men using the narrow double-heddle loom in the northern Yoruba city of Ilorin. Whereas Akwete-derived patterns tend to proceed as a continuous band weft-wise across the textile, Ilorin-derived patterns consist of short repeated pattern elements clearly suggesting their derivation from the products of the narrow loom.

A third style of extra weft patterning is characterised by small repeated motifs, often representing birds, animals and objects of material culture, which are hand-picked through the ground weave. This appears to be particularly associated with Hausa women weavers (see Brigitte Menzel, 1972, for many striking examples) and also with the Nupe, both of northern Nigeria, but there is some suggestion that it could be of Yoruba derivation. Ebira weavers now weave in all three styles and have created within each their own range of patterns. In contrast surviving traditions of Yoruba women's weaving seem to be restricted to simple patterns of warp stripes and the occasional use of openwork, with the exception of the Ijebu cloths discussed above.

The upright single-heddle loom was also found in Benin where it was used by men weavers to produce weft-faced cloth for the king. This was ornamented to a degree of elaboration apparently unmatched elsewhere, with figures of kings and leopards, for use in ceremonial dress (Paula Ben-Amos, 1978). Whether these patterns are made by tapestry weave or by supplementary weft floats is not altogether clear from an examination of the published photographs. Cloth for domestic use was woven by women on the same type of loom throughout the Benin kingdom.

One final area where this particular type of loom evidently thrives is in south-eastern Nigeria among the Ibibio-speaking peoples around the Cross River. Here the weavers using it are all men and the fibre woven is exclusively raphia. The preparation of the fibre is much as in the Zaire Basin (where, incidentally, it is also only men who weave raphia cloth), but, as described in Chapter Two, the individual lengths are knotted together to permit mounting on the loom as a continuous length. The weave which results is generally a balanced plain weave rather than warp faced, and check patterns can be created by introducing stripes of different colour in both warp and weft.

Single-heddle looms employing discrete warp lengths

Ling Roth in his *Studies in Primitive Looms* (1917) opened his discussion of African loom types with a category he called 'The Vertical Mat Loom', the loom most often associated these days with the Zaire Basin. This heading covers upright looms from various parts of Africa which were or had been used in the weaving of raphia cloth. The confusing tendency of earlier writers to gloss as 'matting' any fabric constructed of raphia fibre regardless of what it might actually be used for, has already been observed. The argument being developed here suggests that it is equally misleading to make the nature of the elements woven on a loom, the angle of incline at which a loom is mounted, or indeed the sex of the weaver, the basis of any major taxonomic departures. Certainly raphia cloth is woven on looms other than those which Ling Roth mentions; and, as the loom used is of the single-heddle type, it does not, of course, matter greatly whether it is 'vertical' or not, for the process of weaving remains the same whether it is mounted horizontally or at an oblique angle, as indeed some of these looms are. In the Zaire Basin weaving is a male activity. It is not clear whether this applied in West Africa, where, as we shall see, looms of this kind also occurred.

For all that, we do propose to treat the looms which Ling Roth described as of the vertical mat type as a significant sub-category of the single-heddle loom. Our reason, however, is rather different from his. What is distinctive about this loom, it appears to us, is the system of warping which it employs: the warp is not, as in other examples

Right A Salampasu man, Zaire, weaving on a vertically-mounted single-heddle loom.

Above Men of the Boa people, Welle district, Zaire, attaching the lengths of raphia which will form the warp to a wooden splint prior to mounting it on the loom framework visible to the side.

previously discussed, wound continuously round a set of pegs or beams. Instead the loom employs what might be called discrete warp lengths to indicate the two defining features of this loom: the non-continuous nature of the warp system and the fact that the size of the cloth it produces is determined by the length of the warp elements. (The web or width of the cloth is similarly defined because each pick of the weft is a single length of raphia.) In practice all such looms as they are found in Africa seem to be used in the weaving of raphia cloth, a characteristic which is attributed to the methods by which raphia fibre is prepared. (It will be remembered that a much shorter length of fibre is produced than is the case with other raw materials.) Nevertheless, we do not wish to suggest that all raphia looms must necessarily be of this type. As we know, lengths of raphia may simply be tied end to end to provide a continuous warp and woven on exactly the same looms as are employed in weaving other types of cloth.

The raphia looms which Ling Roth describes all have the system of discrete warp lengths. His examples come from Sierra Leone, south-eastern Nigeria, Cameroun and the Zaire Basin. Their use, however, is and was more widespread. Such looms, for instance, are still found in parts of Angola and Gabon, and their former existence is recorded in Ghana. The presence of such isolated pockets of use throughout West

Africa suggests that the loom may once have had a more comprehensive distribution, as it still does in West Central Africa (see also Lamb, 1982 and 1984). The loom is best known in the Zaire Basin, partly, perhaps, because here it is the only type of loom in traditional use, and because the raphia cloth from this area can be very decorative.

It is the system of warping which is initially distinctive of this type of loom, so our description of it begins with an outline of the method of attaching the warp elements to the loom.

The account of the preparation of the raphia fibre left off at the point where lengths of about one yard had been produced (p. 35). These lengths represented the divided foliole of the raphia leaf, and the folioles had been tied together at one end to form hanks prior to their being split. It is, therefore, as a number of bundles that the warp is presented for mounting on the loom, and in this form they contribute to the whole economy of the process of preparing the loom. Indeed the method of mounting a discontinuous warp need be little more complicated than the simple procedure of winding a continuous warp around the upper and lower beams. The hanks can be simply slipped onto and secured to two batons, and these batons lashed onto the beams of the loom. This is clearly a much more rapid means of setting up the warp than attaching each individual thread in turn: it is also potentially more effective (and it is more like the method of attaching the warp to the beams of a Berber loom than we might have expected). If each warp thread were to be mounted separately variations in length across the warp system would be more difficult to avoid. Where such variations occur they produce unequal tension during the weaving process, and this in its turn produces a cloth with an uneven texture, an effect sometimes desired in European weaving but not in African. However, the procedure of mounting the warp in bundles helps to guarantee the achievement of a more or less even tension when the loom is ready for weaving.

Two weavers of the Yela people, Zaire. The one on the right is drawing the weft through the warp and the one on the left is beating the weft in.

A Kuba weaving hut containing a loom mounted at an oblique angle, as is the custom in this part of Zaire.

The loom is completed by a heddle, a shed stick, and a multi-purpose weaving sword. The heddle also employs several hanks of prepared raphia fibre. Each successive length of fibre picks out an alternate warp element and the two ends of the hank are attached to a wooden baton which stretches across the whole width of the loom. Normally two hanks are enough to pick out all the relevant warp elements. A shed stick is placed between the two groups of warps; and the other basic parts of the loom, the shuttle and the beater-in, are united in one object: the weaving sword. His sword is the weaver's most prized possession. It is a smooth length of hard wood usually shaped into a slight curve, though in parts of Gabon this sword assumes a more exaggerated form. Normally they are undecorated. (An example from the Songye of Zaire which is furnished with a carved head is a rare exception.) As the weft is composed of individual elements the sword is provided with an angled notch at one end into which each successive weft strand can be placed so that it may be passed through the shed or countershed by simply drawing the sword through the passage created by manipulating the heddle and shed stick. The sword is then returned between the warp threads and used to beat in the weft. These, then, are the basic items incorporated into all looms of this type. Divergencies, such as there are, mainly concern the more minor details of the methods by which the warp elements and the leashes of the heddle are attached to their respective batons. These more intricate features of the construction of the loom are dealt with in detail in Hélène Loir's

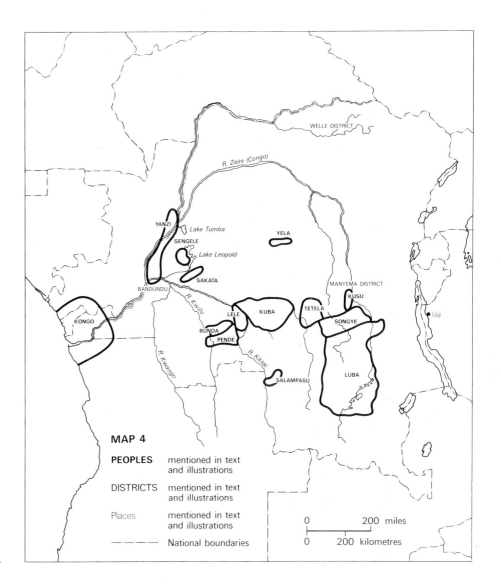

MAP 4

PEOPLES mentioned in text and illustrations

DISTRICTS mentioned in text and illustrations

Places mentioned in text and illustrations

— - — - — National boundaries

0   200 miles

0   200 kilometres

Zaire.

admirable monograph, *Le Tissage du Raphia au Congo Belge* (1935). Variations which are found in the angle at which the loom is mounted, or in the several methods which are used for achieving tension, should be noted, especially as they occur in Zaire, for some of these appear to be particular to this area and to this type of loom.

As a rule these looms are not mounted inside the weaver's house as in other parts of Africa. The loom is generally erected in one of the thoroughfares through a village and in more productive weaving communities is often placed underneath a specially constructed shelter to protect it from the weather. Sometimes more than one loom is found within a single weaving installation and several weavers may be at work at the same time. The need to produce cover for the loom is not perhaps as important as elsewhere because the cloth may take no more than about six hours to weave, and certainly a single day should suffice to complete all but those cloths which contain more intricate designs. Even when no weaving is in process or planned a fixed structure, to which the batons supporting the warp are lashed, usually remains in place. In most parts of West Africa, and all but a few parts of Zaire, this fixed structure consists of a vertical rectangular construction of stout wooden poles. To set up the loom, the horizontal batons are lashed onto the cross-beams, thereby bringing the warp elements into tension. One variation on this method of mounting the loom (and which eluded Ling Roth when he asserted that all looms of this type are set up vertically) occurs in southern Zaire. Here the loom is attached to a fixed structure at an

A man of the Sengele people of the Lake Leopold area of Zaire. He is weaving on the loom of that region, which incorporates a stirrup to enable the weaver to tension the warps.

angle of 45° and the weaver sits beneath the angle of the loom to work. None the less, like the vertical loom, it employs the familiar method of fixed tension.

Amongst the peoples who live round Lakes Leopold and Tumba a method which may be called 'mobile tension' is employed to stretch the warp elements. As before a fixed upright structure is used, but in this case the lower beam is lacking and it is only the upper beam which is tied onto the structure. The lower beam is loose and has a wooden splint or stirrup attached to it by leather thongs. The weaver sits on the ground and to achieve tension he places his feet in the stirrup and pushes outwards and downwards. It is obviously difficult to maintain a constant tension by such means even for the most contortionist of weavers, which, no doubt, explains the limited distribution of such methods. In our experience this, which can be called a footstrap loom, is unique to this small area of north-western Zaire. It is perhaps some indication of its rarity that in the British Museum's collections one such stirrup with its leather thongs attached was, until recently identified, described as a 'Congolese instrument of torture'!

Even if there are several variations in the loom's construction, such as within the relatively restricted area of the Zaire Basin, the basic cloth which these looms produce is fairly uniform. This is not to say that more decorative cloths are not found, for as we shall see shortly some very elaborate designs are produced both during and after weaving and particularly in the southern half of Zaire. The basic cloth is a balanced plain-weave, naturally-coloured square. Sometimes lengths of raphia are introduced which have been exposed to the sun for different periods of time during the early stages of preparing the fibre. This has the effect of producing subtly darker or lighter shades and these show up as patterns on otherwise unpatterned cloths. Cloth occasionally incorporating this refinement was used over a wide area as clothing,

Detail of a raphia textile, Manyema district, Zaire. Panels and strips of red-brown, purple, black and natural colours provide the decorative element in this textile. The side panels are warp-striped but otherwise pieces of cloth dyed a single colour have been used. Width 54 in (137 cm). 1960. Af 20. 141; The Royal Botanical Gardens, Kew.

several squares being sewn together with raphia thread to produce greater lengths where required. Another interesting function which such cloth performed was that of acting as an instrument of exchange especially in areas where a large demand for cloth was assured. In some parts of the south and east of Zaire, for instance, a piece of raphia cloth about twenty-four inches by sixteen inches was used for paying tribute. Such cloth was known as *madiba*. In the area occupied in the main by the Kongo peoples, strips of cloth were bound together in book form and used as currency. Elsewhere, in the Kwango-Kwilu area, raphia cloth was rolled up into tight bundles to act as a medium of exchange and in areas such as these the weaver, as the 'minter' of cloth-money, was a man of considerable prestige.

The weaver's art, however, is best seen in the more elaborate cloths which these looms produce. The use of dyed warp and/or weft elements, of supplementary shed sticks, and even of supplementary heddles are all known. Again it is in Zaire that these refinements are most familiar, and it is here that the most decorative cloths are found. By contrast, those that we know to have been produced on this type of loom in West Africa, though they seem to have employed dyed elements on occasion, appear to have been for the most part plain unpatterned cloths.

We already know of the design possibilities introduced into the weaving process by the use of additional shed sticks. Supplementary weft patterns may be alternately laid in and floated and often emphasised by using darker coloured raphia. The patterns themselves are geometric and repeated along the whole length of the cloth. There is nothing unusual in this. What is distinctive in an area like Zaire is the number of additional shedding devices which are sometimes employed, particularly where more detailed patterns are intended. One example from the Tetela of eastern Zaire in the British Museum collections contains thirty-six supplementary shed sticks.

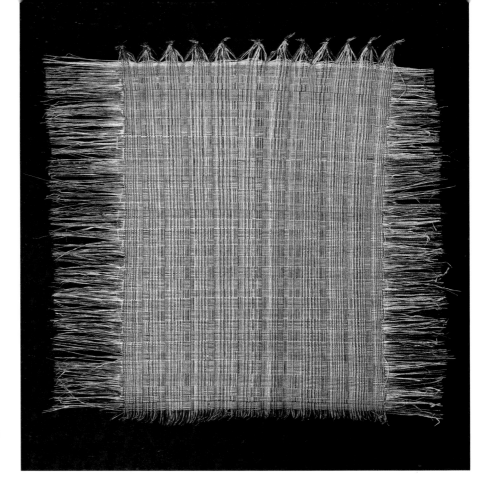

Raphia textile, probably Kusu, Zaire. In this example the use of two alternating colours in both warp and weft enhances the otherwise plain-weave structure.
26 in (65 cm) square. 1955. Af 14. 2;
Mrs G. M. Cartwright.

Opposite Raphia loom, Tetela, Zaire. A single-heddle loom of the conventional kind but with thirty-six supplementary shed sticks used to record the pattern on the already woven section of cloth.
Length 41 in (104 cm). 1909. Ty 822.

The main function of these shed sticks is to act as a mnemonic device. They can be used most effectively where a pattern is required that is made up of two halves, so that one is the reverse of the other – like a lozenge design which, if halved, is seen to be composed of two triangles, the second a mirror image of the first. The shed sticks are used in the following manner: the first half of the pattern has to be picked out by hand. However, as each shed is created and the weft drawn through and beaten in, it is also traced up the warps and a wooden splint, in effect a shed stick, inserted as a record of it. Clearly, by recording the first shed in the sequence at the top of the unwoven section of the warp, and each subsequent shed in order beneath it, the pattern created by the shed sticks will be the exact reverse of that appearing on the woven section of the cloth. When, therefore, the second half of the design is woven, the sheds can be quickly and accurately recreated in reverse order, thereby completing the pattern.

The only drawback with this method of producing supplementary weft patterns occurs where the whole design is to be repeated, for each new section has to be virtually picked out as before. The shed sticks cannot be re-used a second time. The reason for this is that, because other shed sticks remain in place and because the supplementary weft floats overlap, they make it impossible to retrace the shed up the warp and put the shed stick back again above these ready for further use. If a shed stick is not immediately removed after use, it blocks successive sheds from being transferred to the cloth. In practice it is only the last shed stick in any sequence which can be thus recycled.

One way round this difficulty is to use instead of shed sticks only, a combination of supplementary shed sticks and supplementary single-heddles, the latter providing a more permanent record of any desired shed. In the case of the Tetela loom mentioned, with its thirty-six additional shed sticks, supplementary heddles are impractical, because on these looms the warp length is not sufficient to accommodate as many as would be required. For designs requiring fewer shed sticks, however, the use of supplementary single-heddles does provide a simpler means of creating the required design without having to pick each out by hand on every occasion. In Zaire looms incorporating up to six supplementary single-heddles with their associated shed sticks are known.

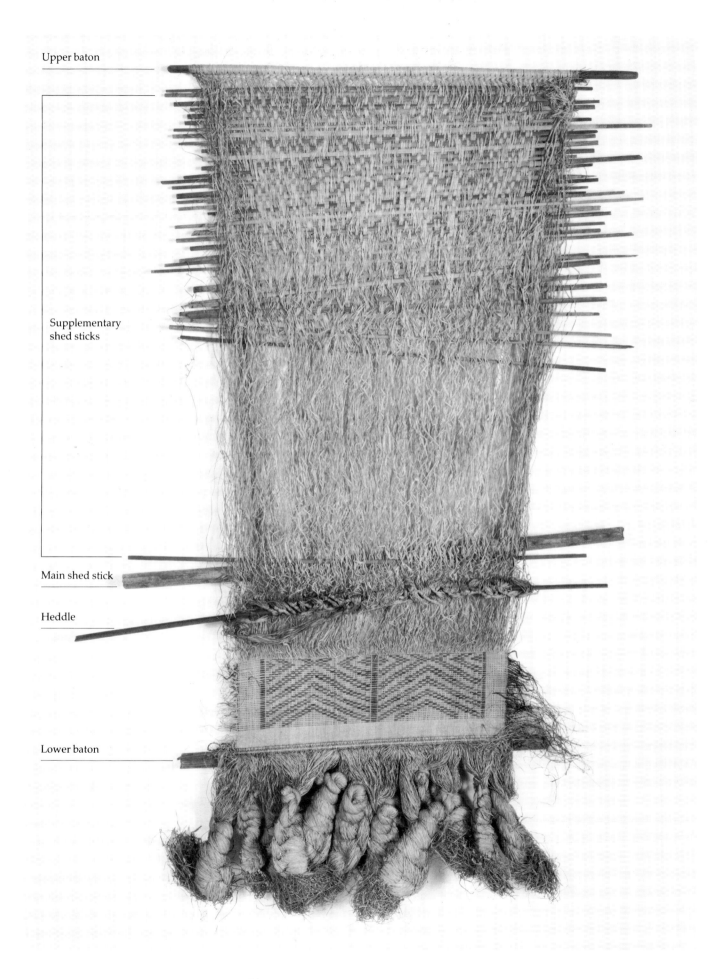

Upper baton

Supplementary
shed sticks

Main shed stick

Heddle

Lower baton

CHAPTER FIVE

THE

DOUBLE-HEDDLE

LOOM

A Yoruba weaver at Oyo, Nigeria. The heddles, beater and pulley of his loom are suspended from a bar which is itself hung from the roof of the lean-to shelter in which the weaver is sitting. This loom was collected for the British Museum.

The mechanical principles of the double-heddle loom have been set out briefly in Chapter Three above. In contrast to the single-heddle loom, both groups of warp elements are leashed to heddles, each group to one of a pair constructed and connected so that one heddle cannot be operated independently of the other. The two therefore work together to form the shed and countershed. We now consider the distribution and variety of form within this class in some detail together with the kinds of fabric woven on them and the decorative embellishments achieved by this mechanism. It should perhaps be noted that any weave or decorative embellishment possible with a single-heddle loom is also possible with the double-heddle, and vice versa. The mechanics of the latter, however, permit the manufacture of cloth at a greater speed than is possible with a single-heddle and shed stick.

The double-heddle loom is found in West and in North-east Africa, i.e. Ethiopia, Somalia, the Sudan and southern Egypt (and it is the loom of urban Arab North Africa). It is thus geographically somewhat more limited in its distribution than the single-heddle loom, although in the two areas mentioned by far the greater volume of cloth is woven on it. The double-heddle loom also occurs among some of the Betsimisaraka of eastern Madagascar, and may once have been more generally distributed.

The particular variety of this loom found in West Africa is generally referred to as a narrow strip loom and even as a belt loom, and in North-east Africa as a pit loom or as a pit-treadle loom. These names do, of course, refer to significant features of this type of loom as it occurs in these areas. They are, on the other hand, misleading in some degree as each is essentially the same as the other in its mechanical principles and as the Middle Eastern looms illustrated by Shelagh Weir (1970). In all of these looms the shedding device is a pair of heddles connected by way of a pulley suspended from above, the warp being mounted more or less horizontally, and attached below to a pair of pedals or treadles operated by the weaver's feet. This leaves his hands free to manipulate the weft, in contrast to the single-heddle loom.

The weaver sits at one end of his apparatus. Immediately in front of him is the breast or cloth beam to which one end of the warp elements is attached and onto which the cloth is rolled as it is woven. A peg through the breast beam to one side prevents it unrolling and thereby releasing the tension on the warp. From the breast beam the warp elements pass through the *reed* or *beater*. This consists of a rectangular frame, wider, obviously, than the cloth woven on the loom. Within this frame are set a great many thin slats (in West Africa of bamboo or palm midrib) between which the warp

Above Another view of the Yoruba loom showing warp beam, pedals, etc. The weaver sits on a mud bench and, unlike the Ethiopian weaver illustrated on p. 95, there is no need for a pit to be dug beneath the loom.

Right Yoruba weavers at Iseyin, Nigeria. Iseyin and Ilorin seem to be the most prolific centres of narrow strip weaving among the Yoruba. Note in this illustration the U-shaped sledges weighed down with stones, which keep the warps in tension.

A weaver of the Konso people of southern Ethiopia. He sits on the edge of the pit in which he operates the pedals of his loom. The warp is tied to a post behind the weaver.

elements pass. The beater is suspended from above and with it the weaver beats in each individual pick of the weft.

Next, the warp elements pass through the pair of heddles, which are suspended and operated as described above (p. 46). In African as in Middle Eastern double-heddle looms each heddle consists of a pair of sticks set parallel to each other. Between them is a series of interlinked loops of string or some other flexible material. These are the leashes and each loop or leash interlinks with its opposite partner so that an *eye* is formed through which one or more warp elements may pass. It follows, therefore, that if the heddle is raised or lowered the warp elements passing through the eyes of its leashes will also be raised or lowered. It also follows that, for the simplest plain weave, in which the interlacing order of warp and weft is over-one/under-one, if a warp element (or unit of elements) passes through the eye of one of the pair of heddles it must pass between the leashes of the other, and vice versa. As successive warp elements or units pass alternately through the eye and between the leashes they are automatically separated into two groups by the heddles, which are arranged one behind the other. If one heddle is pulled down by depressing the pedal attached to it, the other is raised and each group of warp elements lowered or raised accordingly. The mechanical principles are simple in practice though difficult to describe in words.

Finally, the warp elements reach the warp beam. On the European handloom the warp is rolled around the warp beam and unrolled from it as cloth is woven and rolled onto the breast beam. In West Africa the warp usually passes over the warp beam to a *dragstone*; i.e. it is attached to a wooden sledge, or a piece of leather or sheet metal, upon which a heavy stone is placed. The dragstone is heavy enough to apply tension to the warp but not so heavy that it cannot be drawn towards the weaver as weaving progresses and cloth is rolled onto the breast beam. In North-east Africa the warp beam is a stout peg driven vertically into the ground. It is the first of a series of pegs around which the warp is stretched until it reaches a final peg to which it is tied.

Cotton textile, Mende, Sierra Leone. An example of the so-called Njaye cloths, woven of hand-spun yarn, white with indigo supplementary weft patterning, made up of eleven strips. Total width 59 in (150 cm). 1952. Af 20. 4; the Public Relations Officer, Freetown.

Among the Manjaka and Papel peoples of West Africa, and in Madagascar, the warp is also attached to a warp peg in front of the loom; while Mende looms employ an arrangement of the 'raised ground' loom type (see p. 56).

The reason the North-east African double-heddle loom is called a pit loom is because the weaver sits at ground level with his feet operating the pedals (or treadles, hence pit-treadle loom) in a pit dug beneath the loom. The looms Shelagh Weir illustrates are pit looms; and the woman's single-heddle loom of eastern Yorubaland could also be called a pit loom! The term is misleading, therefore, inasmuch as the pit has nothing to do with the basic mechanism of the loom.

The West African loom is called a narrow-strip loom or belt loom simply because of the extraordinary narrowness of the web. The weaving of cloth as narrow as less than one inch is known among the Hausa, although some Hausa weavers are also known to produce cloth on the double-heddle loom as wide as thirty inches. However, most cloth woven on the double-heddle loom in West Africa is between three and ten inches wide; about four inches and about eight inches are particularly common widths. Broader pieces of cloth are made by sewing the strips together, selvedge to selvedge. These strips are not woven in short lengths since the usual practice is to prepare a warp of sufficient length so that when cut up into shorter pieces it will be enough to join together into a single cloth. The weaving of such narrow strips of cloth, whether on a single- or double-heddle loom, is not unknown in other parts of the world (the strips woven for use in and around the Sahara which take the strain of the guy ropes of a tent have already been mentioned), though it is exceedingly unusual and there is no satisfactory explanation of its existence in West Africa as the norm of a vigorous textile industry. There probably is no simple reason and no one factor which can be held to account for it.

The principal yarn woven on the double-heddle loom in West Africa is cotton though wool and silk, and today rayon and lurex, are also woven in many places. West African narrow-strip weaving will be described at length below. In North-east Africa the double-heddle loom appears to be used exclusively for weaving cotton. Wool is also woven but on the single-heddle loom, as described in the previous chapter, and by women; in both West and North-east Africa the double-heddle loom is the almost exclusive property of male weavers. (It does not follow that the single-heddle loom is used exclusively by women: in south-east Nigeria, northern Cameroun and Zaire, and possibly elsewhere, this has been shown not to be the case.) The isolated occurrence of a double-heddle loom in Madagascar will be described in the section dealing with the oddities of Malagasy weaving.

The double-heddle loom in West Africa

Textile design as effected on this loom depends mainly on the relative spacing of warp and weft elements with the introduction of stripes to either or both sets, and the use of supplementary weft floats; and we also, less frequently, find examples of tapestry weave, weft inserts and openwork. Our purpose is to show something of the variety of pattern and texture achieved with a relatively restricted range of weave structures. We shall describe very briefly a number of distinct weaving traditions beginning with the Mende of Sierra Leone, proceeding along the River Niger via the Fulani, Djerma and others to the Yoruba and Hausa peoples of Nigeria and thence to the Asante and Ewe of Ghana among whom the greatest development of technical virtuosity is reached in West Africa. Finally we mention the one case of European-influenced textile design, the weaving of the Manjaka and Papel peoples of Guinea-Bissau. This selection of cultures to some extent depends on the particular strengths of the collections of the British Museum. There are important weaving traditions in Senegal, Ivory Coast and Burkina Faso, for example, which are unrepresented in the collections and the textile industries of the middle and upper Niger are also barely represented; they are discussed here because it would be impossible to begin a comprehensive picture of West African weaving otherwise. The collection of Alastair and Venice Lamb was the other major collection of West African textiles in England, a collection strongest where the Museum's collections are weakest. It has been illustrated by

Cotton hammock, Mende or Sherbro, Sierra Leone. Woven on the man's double-heddle loom of hand-spun yarn in weft-faced strips about 9 in (23 cm) wide, with small areas of float weave and supplementary weft patterns. (The Mende also weave warp-striped cloths in strips about 4 in (10 cm) wide.) Length 87 in (221 cm). 1934. 3–7. 183; Beving Collection.

Venice Lamb in her book *West African Weaving* (1975) and is now in the collections of the Smithsonian Institution, Washington, D.C.

Before proceeding further, it is perhaps worth saying that plain white or indigo-dyed cloth, woven of either hand- or machine-spun cotton yarn, is the ubiquitous product of West African looms. Despite the fact that we, in common with other writers in this field, concentrate on design and pattern, it should not be forgotten that possibly the greater volume of cloth produced in West Africa is plain white.

Mende weaving: Weavers of the Mende people of Sierra Leone manufacture cloth in two distinct widths, about four inches and about eight inches wide, using hand-spun yarn in both cases. Both are woven on the same type of loom (the special features of which will be discussed later in this chapter).

The narrower strip is either a balanced plain weave, fairly loosely woven, or it tends towards a warp-faced structure. Cloths sewn together from these strips may be white, or sometimes they may be dyed indigo or brown after completion. There are also many patterns of warp stripes in different shades of indigo, natural or dyed brown and white. Cloths are woven in a similar range of patterns of stripes and of colours

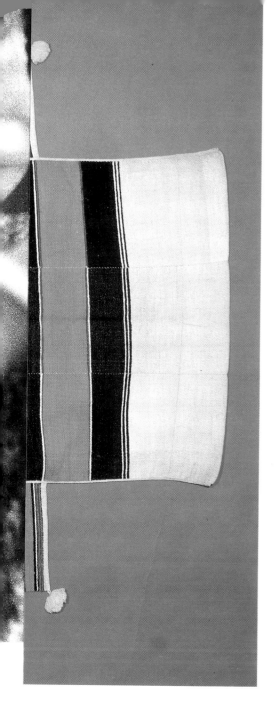

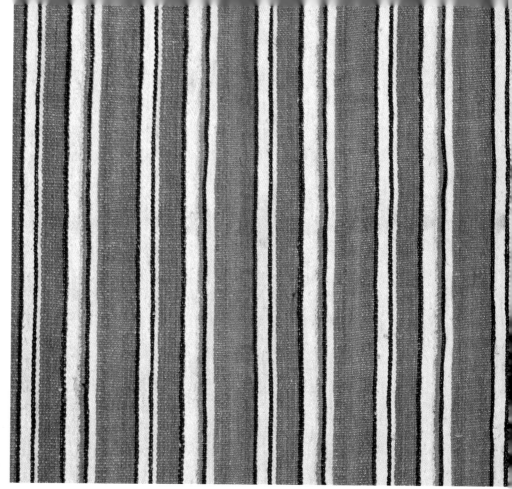

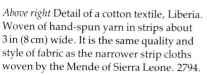

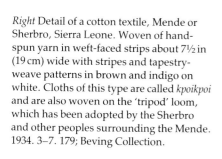

Above right Detail of a cotton textile, Liberia. Woven of hand-spun yarn in strips about 3 in (8 cm) wide. It is the same quality and style of fabric as the narrower strip cloths woven by the Mende of Sierra Leone. 2794.

Right Detail of a cotton textile, Mende or Sherbro, Sierra Leone. Woven of hand-spun yarn in weft-faced strips about 7½ in (19 cm) wide with stripes and tapestry-weave patterns in brown and indigo on white. Cloths of this type are called *kpoikpoi* and are also woven on the 'tripod' loom, which has been adopted by the Sherbro and other peoples surrounding the Mende. 1934. 3–7. 179; Beving Collection.

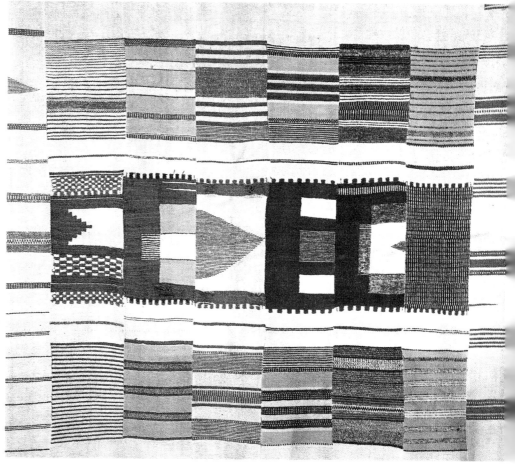

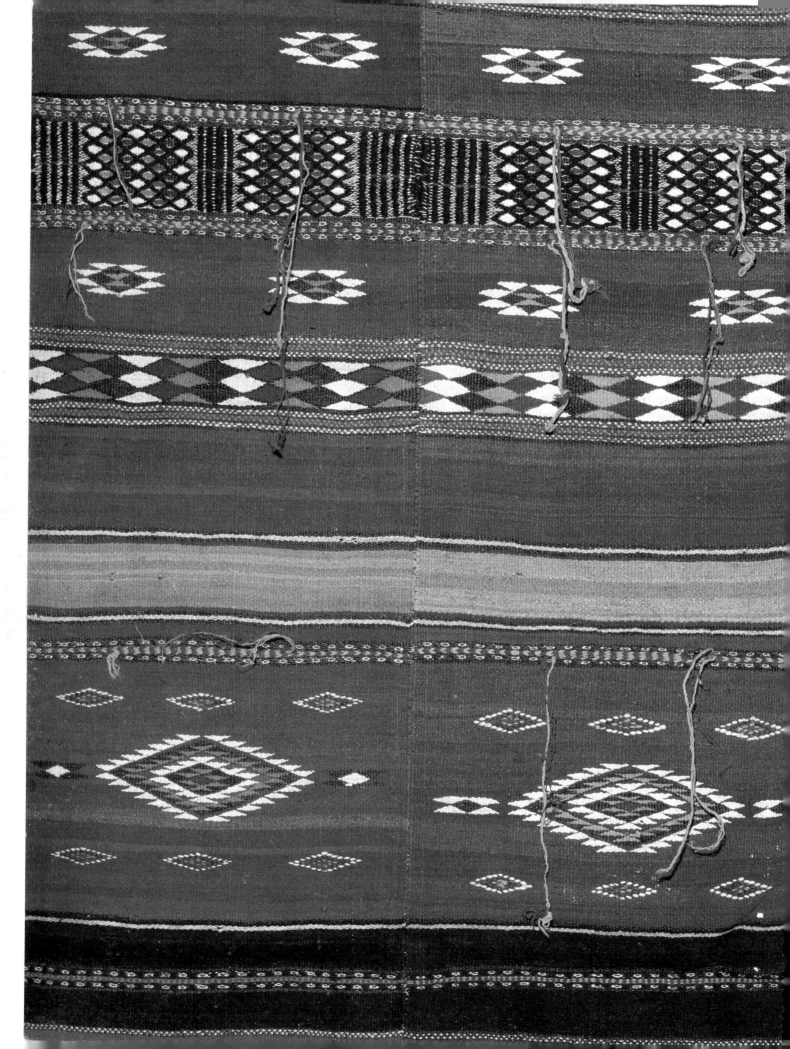

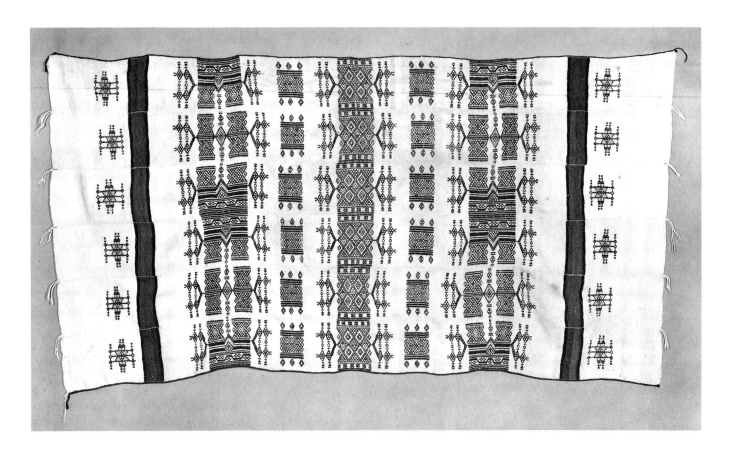

Woollen blanket, Fulani, Mali. Woven of sheep's wool in weft-faced strips about 8 in (20 cm) wide, with stripes and extra weft patterns in red and black on white. This is an example of the *khasa* commissioned by nomadic Fulani but traded second-hand all over West Africa. Courtesy Joan Wescott.

the end of the season a blanket may be sold to local cloth traders unless it is of particularly high quality. There is, as a result, an enormous quantity of used blankets in circulation. The principal cloth market in the area is at Mopti where merchants buy and sell second-hand blankets and employ large numbers of men to launder them and repair holes, tears and defects. From Mopti, second-hand *khasa* are traded to many other parts of West Africa.

Wool and cotton are spun and dyed by women and can be purchased in the market. When a man wishes to order a blanket it is his responsibility to purchase the necessary yarn and see to the laying of the warp. In the past both warp and weft were of woollen yarn but around the turn of the century, according to Imperato (1973), cotton replaced wool for the warp elements. The blankets are themselves usually six to eight feet in length and consist of six strips, each with a web of around eight inches, sewn selvedge to selvedge. Following upon a consideration of Mende and Bamana weaving, as we might now begin to expect in a strip of this width, the cloth is weft-faced.

Each area of the inland delta has its own particular style, or range of styles, and quality of blanket, and *khasa* are only woven to order. Conformity to local tradition is expected of a weaver by his clients and these blankets display none of the diversity found in other textiles woven by the Fulani.

The simplest (and presumably cheapest) blankets are plain white. Pattern may be added by means of weft stripes in red, yellow or black, as well as by supplementary wefts principally in black but with occasional dashes of red, yellow and cotton-white. These weft floats are woven in to form distinctive patterns of lozenges, triangles, chevrons, lines and spots. Particular combinations of these are, according to Imperato, identified with aspects of the transhumant herder's environment, including topography, the homestead, women and brothers, and there are named standard combinations of stripes and weft-float patterns which make up the complete blanket.

As the patterns are weft-wise and must match up when the stripes are sewn together, the weaver must pay careful attention to the spacing of the various designs.

He may use finger, hand or arm lengths, or a small measuring stick. The 'traditional' measuring rod, still used for cloth outside the main centres of commerce, appears to be around one cubit in length.

Plain white blankets may also be turned into a man's gown by folding them in half, partially stitching along the sides and opening up a hole for the wearer's neck at the centre. So constructed these gowns may sometimes be dyed dark brown.

Imperato (1976) also describes another kind of Fulani woollen cloth, about fifteen feet in length and made of seven strips, each about thirteen inches wide. It is weft-faced with a range of colour and pattern quite unlike and altogether more magnificent than the familiar *khasa*. These cloths are both rarely woven and expensive. Renée Boser-Sarivaxévanis (1975), figure 8) illustrates one of these hung in front of a marriage bed at Niafounke at the northern end of the inland Niger delta. The colours include red-brown, yellow, black and white woven in simple weft stripes and tapestry weave with supplementary weft floats.

Fulani weavers manufacture many other kinds of cloth of wool and of cotton, as well as in the two combined, and make use of the wide range of factory-dyed colours which are now available, in addition to local vegetable dyes. Unfortunately little is published to indicate the full range of Fulani textiles, nor the extent to which the ranges of textiles woven by different peoples in this area overlap one with another. For example, Renée Boser-Sarivaxévanis (1972b) illustrates as Fulani, a textile very similar to one identified by Imperato (1974) as Bamana.

Finally, in our consideration of Fulani weaving it should be mentioned that some of the textiles discovered in the Tellem caves of the Bandiagara escarpment of Mali were probably woven by the Fulani. They are associated with archaeological material dated to the eleventh century and earlier. Both cotton and woollen yarn are employed. Some of them are weft-faced strips with a web of seven inches and with patterns of stripes and small bands of supplementary weft floats. Others are narrower with a web of around four inches and stripes in both warp and weft. A selection of these cloths is illustrated and described by Venice Lamb (1975).

Another pattern of cloth similar to the marriage-bed cloth described above, and probably the more attractive visually, is illustrated by Sieber (1972, p. 190) and Menzel (1972, vol. III, no. 45); and the British Museum is fortunate in having acquired an example of it. The fabric is weft-faced, woven of goat hair and sheep's wool in a strip about thirteen inches wide. The range of colours is much as before though without any large white areas. It is predominantly red-brown with weft stripes and tapestry weave, in black, yellow, blue and cotton-white and some areas of supplementary weft floats in black. These cloths are described as tent dividers and marriage-bed hangings used by the pastoral people of the area. Their similarity of style with the cloths previously mentioned might lead one to expect that they too are woven by the Fulani of the inland Niger delta. They are in fact woven at Tillaberi, further downstream in Niger (although this tells us nothing about the identity of the weavers themselves who may still be Fulani). In the 1970s, Venice and Alastair Lamb found that, with the scarcity of wool and goat hair, the weavers at Tillaberi now produced copies in imported, ready-dyed cotton. This particular textile provides the closest parallel in terms of pattern with some of the weaving of the Berber tribes of North Africa. A particularly striking example is a blanket (illustrated in Eydoux, 1934) said to be from the Gourara region of the north-western Sahara, in Algeria. Although woven on a Berber single-heddle loom, presumably of the upright variety, in the broad width typical of Berber weaving, there is a very close correspondence in the form and style of the tapestry-weave patterning.

Somewhat different is the tent divider from Goundam, west of Timbuktu, illustrated by Venice Lamb (1975, p. 43). It is woven of woollen yarn in strips no more than four inches wide. The weave is weft-faced and the basic design consists of alternating squares of white and deep indigo, giving a chessboard-like effect when sewn together; and groups of squares at intervals along the cloth have woven into them narrower weft stripes of red-brown and yellow together with tapestry-weave triangles, chevrons and lozenges. Rene Gardi (1969, plate 158) illustrates a cloth woven in the same

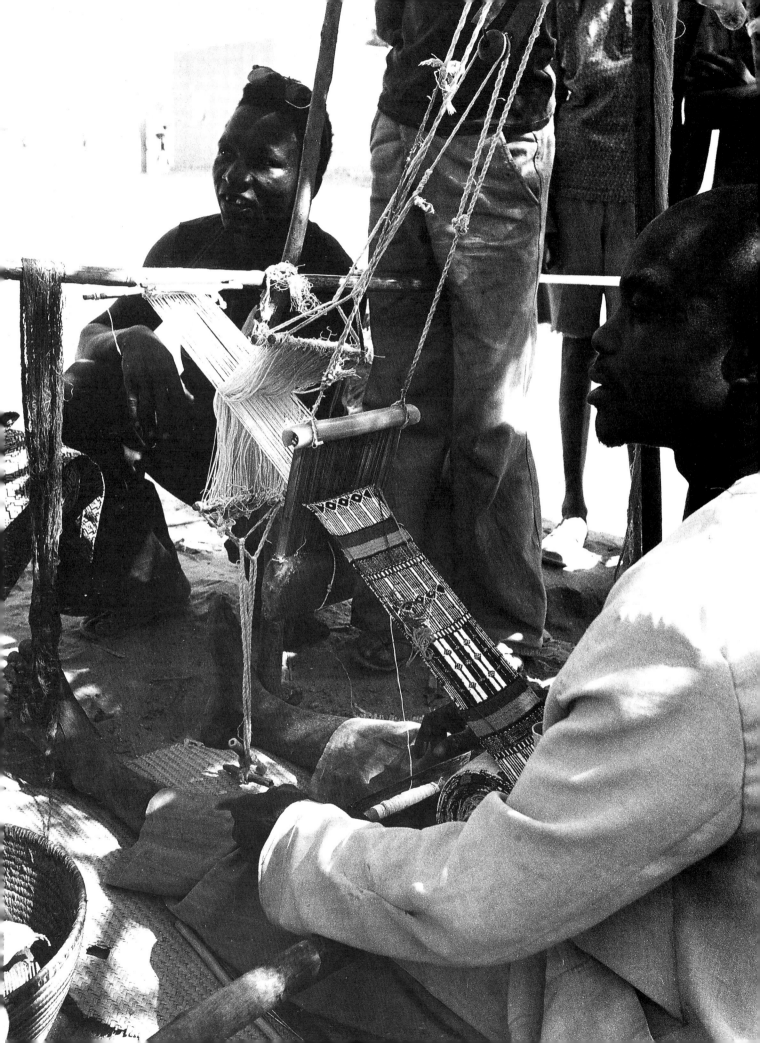

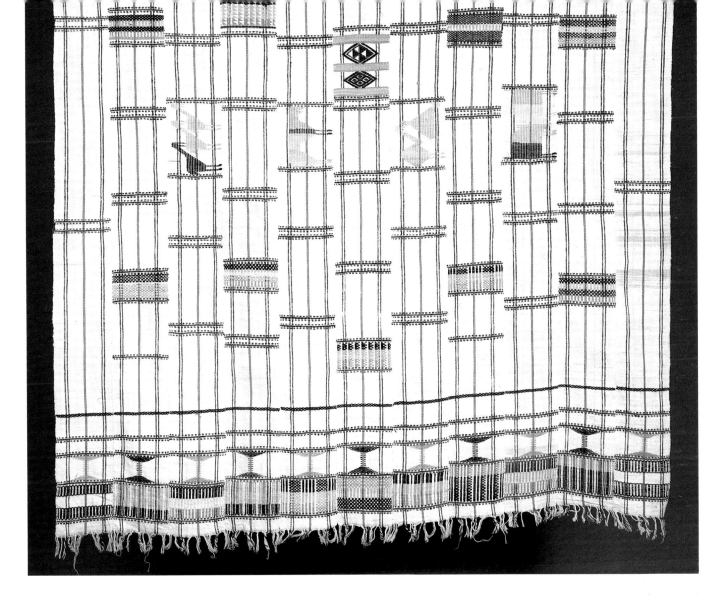

Above Detail of a cotton textile, Djerma, Burkina Faso. Woven principally of hand-spun yarn in 4½ in (11.4 cm) balanced-weave strips with indigo and red stripes in the warp and indigo, red, green and yellow supplementary weft-float patterns. The red yarn is machine-spun. This cloth was collected by the donor at Obuasi, Ghana, although it was probably woven at Dori in eastern Burkina Faso, by weavers of the Djerma people. 1937. 10–2. 4; Captain R. P. Wild.

Opposite A Djerma weaver at Niamey, Niger. He is weaving the complex weft-float patterns typical of Niamey cloth using a pair of supplementary single-heddles which, in this photograph, can be seen just before the warp beam.

manner hung from a Tuareg tent in the area north of Gao to the east of Timbuktu. Venice Lamb illustrates another cloth also composed of weft-faced strips with a web of around four inches, although woven of cotton and in squares of black, white, green, red and yellow (1975, p. 41). It was collected at Gao, although it could equally well have been purchased at Bamako (one place among others where it could have been woven), Ouagadougou or Niamey. However, together with others of similar structure, the identity of the weavers of these narrower-width weft-faced cloths and many other cloth types circulating in this area is unknown for lack of appropriate field research, although it may well be that many of them are woven by Songhai weavers originating in the country around Timbuktu.

Djerma weaving: Whether a textile is warp-faced or weft-faced depends on the relative spacing of the two sets of elements. This, in practice, depends partly upon how the warp is mounted on the loom: the more the individual elements are spaced out the less they will predominate. Djerma weavers, however, in the region of Niamey sometimes combine two simple weave structures in one strip of cloth. A balanced weave structure of white machine-spun cotton about four inches wide is broken at intervals by broad weft-faced stripes in various colours. This is achieved by grouping the individual warp elements into units of four (which effectively reduces the number of warps per inch to wefts per inch) and by doubling the thickness of the weft yarn employed at this point. The novelty of alternating two simple weave structures in one length of cloth is visually obscured by incorporating these weft-faced stripes into pattern areas otherwise formed by continuous supplementary weft floats in black and red which are consistently overshot so that one face of the textile is the negative of the other. Another textile, acquired by the British Museum in 1934 and identified as 'Fulani' in the Accessions Register, but as Djerma by Gabus (1955, p. 53), has a rather different style of embellishment. It is composed of hand-spun cotton with narrow weft-wise stripes in between which human and animal figures are woven by means of discontinuous supplementary weft floats.

Hausa and Nupe weaving: Among the Hausa and Nupe peoples of northern Nigeria both men and women manufacture textiles. The woman's loom has already been described: it is the upright single-heddle loom. If a man is a weaver, however, he works at the double-heddle loom. In the Kano region, several widths of cloth are woven; for example, an extremely narrow strip of white, balanced-weave cotton often less than one inch wide; strips often with patterns of stripes in the warp and sometimes also in the weft of about two inches wide, of about four inches wide, and another between twenty and thirty inches wide; and a weft-faced strip about eight inches wide. A weaver will specialise exclusively in weaving cloth of one or other of these types. Much of this cloth, including any with silk, is in fact the work of Nupe weavers domiciled in Hausa communities (Perani, 1989).

Most Nupe patterns of stripes are typically in various shades of indigo in combination with each other and with white, and occasionally other colours. Many shades of brown, red, yellow and green were also available. Popular colours of machine-spun yarn seem to be maroon, yellow and green. Indigo ikat-dyed yarn is also sometimes used in the warp. Wild silk, *tsamiya*, which is a pale greyish-brown colour, was combined in the warp with a cotton stripe to weave certain prestige fabrics but its use is now increasingly rare. During the nineteenth and early twentieth century magenta waste silk imported from Europe in the trans-Sahara trade was spun and woven and combined with indigo-dyed and white cotton. A large quantity of plain white cloth is woven by Hausa weavers. Whatever the pattern of stripes, however, the principal use of these textiles is for clothing. The strips are cut and sewn together selvedge to selvedge to form pieces of cloth suitable for the various types of garment worn by the Hausa which are described and illustrated in the final chapter, dealing with embroidery. The narrowest strip is used in the manufacture of turban cloths (p. 147).

The weft-faced strips, which are woven only of cotton, are cut and sewn together to make blankets. Pattern is created by weft stripes and inserts. These blankets are easily confused with similar fabrics woven elsewhere in West Africa. One diagnostic feature is the incorporation of elongated triangular weft inserts projecting in from the selvedge part of the way across the cloth. These particular motifs are referred to as 'knives', in Hausa and Nupe embroidery.

Yoruba weaving: There are many similarities between Yoruba and Nupe weaving, which is hardly surprising given that Nupe weavers claim to be of Yoruba origin (Nadel, 1946). Both sexes, for example, manufacture textiles, women on the upright single-heddle loom for domestic use and men on the double-heddle loom as a professional skill.

Cloth is woven by Yoruba men in a strip about four inches wide. As among the Nupe, the strip is, of course, cut and sewn together selvedge to selvedge to make various garments: wrap-around cloths and headscarves for women, and gowns, trousers and caps for men. It is a semi-luxury product as it is more expensive than the cheapest imported cotton cloths and also has, in fact, to compete with the more expensive imported fabrics such as velvet, damask, lace and so on.

Some facts and figures are available for the town of Iseyin in the south-west of the Oyo Kingdom. Iseyin is one of the principal centres of men's double-heddle weaving in Yorubaland. It was estimated (Dodwell, 1955) that in 1953 out of a total population of nearly 50,000 people as many as one in five of the adult males were weavers, manufacturing around one million square yards of cloth a year. The vast majority of weavers between the ages of sixteen and forty were whole-time professionals. A few, in addition to working at the loom, did some trading in cloth or yarn, or some Koranic teaching (almost all Iseyin weavers are Muslim). None admitted to farming as a part-time occupation. Many other people in Iseyin, in addition to the weavers, are also engaged in the textile industry: cloth merchants, yarn sellers, spinners, dyers and so

Yoruba weavers, Nigeria. On the loom in the foreground the shed stick has opened up the warps to permit the passage of a supplementary floating weft.

forth. In 1966 the population had grown to 60,000 and it was estimated that although only around 5 per cent of the adult males were full-time weavers, a further 20 per cent weave from time to time (Bray, 1968).

Three qualities of cloth were woven at Iseyin in 1953. The first was a heavyweight cloth entirely of hand-spun yarn. This accounted for no more than 3 per cent of the total production. The second was a middleweight fabric of mixed hand- and machine-spun cotton, and this accounted for 16 per cent of the total amount of the cloth woven. The third was a lightweight textile entirely of machine-spun yarn which accounted for 81 per cent. Dodwell notes that 20 per cent of the imports of cotton yarn into Nigeria in 1953 was consumed by the Iseyin weaving industry. One of the advantages of machine-spun yarn is that it is easier and quicker to weave (as hand-spun yarn has a rougher surface it tends to catch more readily during the process of weaving.) Dodwell estimated that a weaver's daily average using hand-spun yarn was less than one square yard compared with up to two square yards using machine-spun yarn.

Yoruba cloth varies between the balanced and the more or less warp-faced plain weave. (This applies equally to women's weaving although it is the product of the man's double-heddle loom with which we are concerned here.) As among the Nupe, stripes in various shades of indigo and white are typical, as well as ikat-dyed yarn, and some patterns also introduce a stripe into the weft, partly hidden by the predominant warp. Many warp-stripe patterns are probably shared by Yoruba and Nupe weavers, although beyond this common range the Yoruba appear to be more adventurous particularly with regard to the colours and textures available in machine-spun cotton,

109

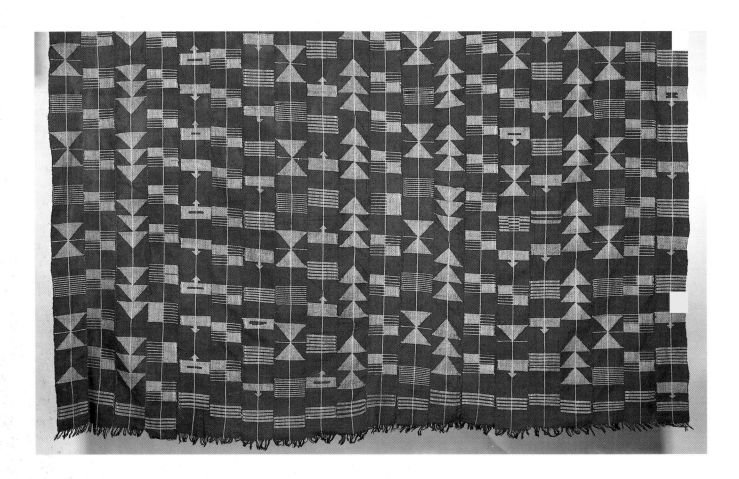

Above Detail of a cotton and rayon textile, Yoruba, Nigeria. Woven of machine-spun cotton with rayon supplementary weft patterns in the manner typical of Ilorin in northern Yorubaland, and composed of twenty strips about 4½ in (11 cm) wide. The donor obtained this cloth at Obuasi in Ghana. Total width 89 in (226 cm), length 10 ft (305 cm). 1937. 12–7. 2; Captain R. P. Wild.

Right Detail of a cotton, lurex and rayon textile, Yoruba, Nigeria. Woven of machine-spun cotton with lurex in the warp, openwork and rayon supplementary weft floats. The strips are approximately 3 in (9 cm) wide. 1987. Af 5. 8.

Far right Detail of a cotton textile, Yoruba. Woven on the man's double-heddle loom of two shades of indigo-dyed hand-spun yarn with machine-spun white yarn in ten strips each about 4 in (10 cm) wide. The total dimensions of the cloth are: width 39 in (99 cm), length 68 in (173 cm). It was probably so made to be a woman's wrap-around skirt. 1934. 3–7. 152; Beving Collection.

rayon and lurex. Dodwell (1955) reports that at Iseyin the demands for the different patterns of warp stripes differs from one part of Yorubaland to another. The local demand was for the more traditional patterns of dark indigo and traders from the southern Yoruba kingdoms of Ijebu also preferred the darker blues. (Both hand-spun and machine-spun cotton yarn is dyed with indigo.) In Ibadan and Lagos, however, there was a preference for lighter colours and combinations of red, beige, and yellow. All the various patterns of stripes are identified by individual names. In some cases the association of name with patterns is probably quite arbitrary. In others, however, the name describes some feature of the pattern to the weaver. For example: 'guinea fowl' (a deep indigo cloth with narrow white stripes in both warp and weft identified with the speckled plumage of that bird); 'plain cloth with one stripe'; 'something which has white'; 'yam porridge which has red in it', and so forth (Eicher, 1976).

In addition to patterns of stripes and the use of ikat-dyed yarn there are other methods employed by Yoruba weavers to embellish their cloth. One of these is openwork (already described for the single-heddle loom), where regular patterns of holes are created by binding small groups of warp elements together using either the ground weft or supplementary wefts. A pastiche openwork can be produced with a comb or similar implement inserted through the warp to disturb the regular position of both warp and weft. After the cloth has been washed a few times, however, holes made in this way look like careless weaving.

Another method is by the use of supplementary weft floats, now usually of rayon on a cotton or mixed cotton/lurex ground weave. J. D. Clarke writing in 1938 said, however, that coloured silk yarn had only been imported during the previous five years and was being used by weavers in place of hand-spun white cotton although at an earlier date European magenta waste silk was also used for supplementary weft-float patterns in Nigeria (though not necessarily by the Yoruba: the Ipswich Museum collections, for example, include a cotton cloth embellished with magenta silk supplementary weft-float Koran board patterns obtained by Charles Partridge at the Igala town of Idah in 1913 where it was said to be of Hausa origin). This technique is the well-known and particular speciality of Ilorin in northern Yorubaland. The extra weft is laid in with the ground weft and floated across one face of the cloth to make the patterns. On the other face, the supplementary weft is not visible for, when it is laid in with the ground weft they are both hidden by the warp-faced structure. In any case, the extra weft is discontinuous; it is worked back and forth only within the pattern area.

Supplementary weft patterns are woven in simple geometric shapes which can be recognised as Koran boards, stools, combs and other domestic objects. To form these patterns a series of supplementary single-heddles and a short flat shed stick are used to raise those warp elements under which the extra weft passes and keep down those over which it floats.

Coloured silk and rayon have been available to the Yoruba weaver for nearly fifty years and yet their main use is at Ilorin and then only for the supplementary weft patterns. In the warp, silk or rayon are used sparingly if at all: the Yoruba double-heddle loom collected for the British Museum at Oyo in 1971 had a thin yellow rayon stripe in an otherwise mainly blue cotton warp. The use of lurex, combined with cotton for the warp, became popular in the late 1970s.

The silk previously available to the Yoruba weaver was the indigenous, pale greyish-brown, wild variety called *sanyan*, used to weave a prestigious cloth of the same name. Today it is rarely woven, a fake version being made of beige-coloured cotton instead. The magenta waste silk exported from Europe via the trans-Saharan trade routes was also popular at one time and widely used by Yoruba weavers in combination with indigo-dyed cotton.

The training of weavers at Iseyin and the marketing of the cloth woven there are described by Dodwell (1955) and Jennifer Bray (1968).

A unique style of supplementary weft patterning, unrelated to anything described above, is provided by the funeral cloths woven among the Bunnu, one of the small Yoruba-speaking tribes of the Kabba region of Nigeria. These cloths were used for wrapping the corpses of wealthy men, for display on the roofs of their houses at their funeral rites, and for masquerade costumes. The ground weave is of white hand-spun cotton using multiple weft units (i.e. several lengths of yarn passed through the same shed), which makes the fabric unusually heavy. Across one face of the cloth, totally obscuring the ground weave, is floated a series of fairly simple geometric patterns in red and beige, with the occasional use of white, yellow, indigo or black. The red is said to be unravelled hospital blanket, the beige is natural brown cotton, the indigo is of coarse home-dyed yarn and the black, white and yellow are machine-spun factory-dyed yarn. The web is narrow, about eight and a half inches. Unfortunately, it is not clear exactly who manufactured them or on what kind of loom. Almost all the weaving in this area is by women using the upright, single-heddle loom and this applies not only to the Yoruba-speaking peoples of the Kabba area, but also to their neighbours to the south, Ebira, and Akoko-Edo and other Northern Edo peoples (all of whom make use of Bunnu funeral cloths but do not weave them). The only other known exception in this area of Nigeria is provided by the village of Ogori, between Ebira and the Northern Edo. Here a prestige cloth is manufactured by specialist male weavers which has a web of twelve inches and is weft-faced with the occasional use of extra weft floats. It is a style of weaving that resembles the weft-faced cotton blankets woven by the Hausa and may have come into this area via the Nupe who conquered it in the late nineteenth century. Bunnu funeral cloths and Ogori weaving do not resemble each other in any way, however.

Asante weaving: The alternation of plain weave structures within one strip of cloth, as found in Djerma weaving, is particularly well developed among Asante, and also Ewe, weavers of Ghana: it is this which gives the distinctive character to much of their weaving. Both peoples also use warp striping and supplementary weft floats. The basic structure is warp-faced and to produce the weft-faced areas a second pair of heddles groups the warp elements into units of six, thus effectively reducing the number of warps to wefts. There are good accounts of the Asante double-heddle loom and its products published by Venice Lamb (1975), Brigitte Menzel (1972) and R. S. Rattray (1972).

Both cotton and silk are woven throughout Asante, cotton for general use and silk for ceremonial use by kings, chiefs and other notables. The weaving of silk, however, is the speciality of the village of Bonwire about twelve miles from the Asante capital, Kumase. Cotton weaving is said to have been introduced in the seventeenth century from the Bondoukou area (now in the Ivory Coast) to the north-west. The unravelling of imported silk cloths in order to incorporate the yarn thus obtained probably began soon after and was noted in the early eighteenth century. Cotton was planted, harvested and spun by women. However, because it takes longer to spin than to weave a given quantity of yarn, a shortage of hand-spun yarn together with the desire for certain colours for which there were no satisfactory local equivalents led to the unravelling of European cottons (Johnson, 1978). Eventually cotton and silk came to be imported ready-spun in skeins. Silk has, of course, now been replaced by rayon.

In order to lay the warp the yarn must be wound onto bobbins, which are made of short lengths of bamboo. Machine-spun and dyed hand-spun yarn is wound onto bobbins from some kind of simple revolving framework; undyed hand-spun yarn can be wound onto the bobbins directly from the spindle. The bobbins are next placed on a bobbin carrier, which is a length of palm midrib with a series of pegs set in it slender enough to take the bobbins. Between two and twelve bobbins, always an even number, may be placed on the bobbin carrier at one time.

The yarn can now be wound around a series of posts, about three feet high, which are set in the ground. The distance between the posts at each end of the series is the maximum length of the strips woven though if a shorter length is required the yarn can simply be wound around fewer posts. At one end of the series either the post is forked or two posts are set close to each other; and between these two branches or posts each individual element is crossed over. This crossing fixes the order in which the warp elements are laid and, therefore, the pattern of stripes, if any. When sufficient warp has been laid the different colours are tied together at the crossing to

Right Preparing (or laying) the warp at Bonwire, the main centre of Asante weaving, near Kumase, Ghana.

Above The crossing over of the warp elements between the fork in the post at one end of the series around which the yarn is wound; Asante, Ghana.

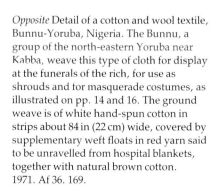

Opposite Detail of a cotton and wool textile, Bunnu-Yoruba, Nigeria. The Bunnu, a group of the north-eastern Yoruba near Kabba, weave this type of cloth for display at the funerals of the rich, for use as shrouds and for masquerade costumes, as illustrated on pp. 14 and 16. The ground weave is of white hand-spun cotton in strips about 84 in (22 cm) wide, covered by supplementary weft floats in red yarn said to be unravelled from hospital blankets, together with natural brown cotton. 1971. Af 36. 169.

preserve the sequence. At Bonwire laying the warp is the work of a specialist other than the weaver himself. Among the Yoruba, in contrast, laying the warp is the work of an apprentice weaver and the yarn is laid around a series of short pegs set in the ground also using a bobbin carrier. Elsewhere in West Africa a set of pegs hammered into the wall of a house may be used. Whatever the differences of detail, however, the basic procedure is the same in all cases.

Laying the warp begins at the post at the opposite end of the series from the crossing. The ends of the yarn on the bobbin carrier are knotted together and looped over the posts. The yarn is then wound around the posts several elements at a time according to the number of bobbins, but in order to make the crossing each element is looped individually between and around the crossing posts. If, to use Rattray's example, the bobbin carrier has six bobbins on it, two with white yarn and four with black, by the time the yarn has passed around the posts, crossed over, and back again a total of four white and eight black elements will have been laid. (Warp-stripe patterns are reckoned by Asante weavers in units of four.) The finest silk cloth strips might have as many as around five hundred warp elements, but a coarser cloth only half that number. When sufficient warp is laid and the crossing tied together, the warp is slipped off the posts and rolled up around a short flat stick, notched at each end, leaving the crossing end of the warp outermost.

Now the weaver must pass the warp through heddles and beater. The typical Asante loom has two pairs of heddles. The pair nearest the weaver is called *asatia*, and is used for weaving the basic warp-faced strip. The pair furthest from the weaver is called *asanan*, and are used for weaving the weft-faced bands and also the supplementary weft floats. The *asanan* heddles are threaded first. To do this the loops at the crossing end are cut a few elements at a time to allow them to be threaded through. One heddle is placed on top of the other. Warp elements are passed through the *asanan* heddles in units of six, and clearly each unit must pass through an eye of one heddle and between the leashes of the other, alternately. Next the warp elements are

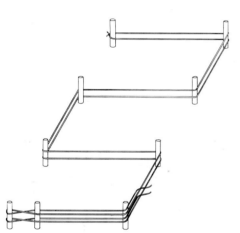

Laying the warp.

passed one by one through the *asatia* heddles. It is the grouping of several elements into a single unit by the *asanan* heddles which reverses the spatial relationship of warp and weft and permits the weaving of weft-faced areas in an otherwise warp-faced cloth. Finally the warp elements are threaded through the beater, this time in units of two, three or four.

There are two further pieces of equipment, the shed stick and the shuttle. The shed stick is a small flat piece of wood used when the weaver wishes to manipulate the *asanan* heddles by hand rather than switching his feet between two sets of pedals. If a heddle is depressed by hand the shed stick can be inserted to open up the shed to permit the passage of a supplementary weft. When inserting a supplementary weft in addition to the ground weft this method is quicker than shifting one's feet continually back and forth from one set of pedals to the other. The shuttle is a boat-shaped piece of wood in which a bobbin is mounted so that it can spin freely allowing the yarn to unwind as it passes through the warp.

The apparatus is now ready to be mounted on the loom framework, which in Asante is often carefully carpentered. The heddles are suspended by means of a pair of heddle pulleys which, together with the beater, are suspended from the top of the loom framework. A cord attached to the bottom of each heddle enables it to be pulled down. At the end of each of these cords is a calabash disc which enables the weaver to grip the cord between his toes.

In order to attach the warp to the cloth beam the ends of the warp, which were cut so that they could be threaded through the heddles and the beater, are knotted together again. A short stick called a *heading rod* is passed through the loops thus formed and is then tied to the breast beam. At the far side of the loom framework the warp is passed over the warp beam. A substantial length of warp is unrolled and attached to the dragstone sledge with another heading rod. Weaving may now begin.

Right An Asante weaver at Bonwire near Kumase, Ghana. Note the calabash disc pedals, the carpentered framework and especially the two pairs of heddles, each suspended from a pulley. The pair nearest to the weaver is used for the warp-faced ground weave while the second pair is used for the weft-faced areas and supplementary float patterns.

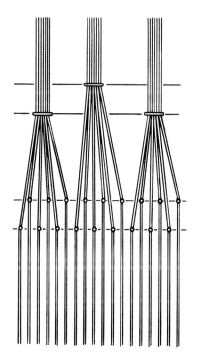

Asante and Ewe weavers thread the warp through the two pairs of heddles in the manner shown here.

The bulk of Asante weaving was in cotton, particularly fine cotton locally hand-spun or imported from northern Ghana, and there is an enormous number of different patterns of warp stripes mostly in indigo of various shades, and white. These are thought by Venice Lamb to derive from the weaving tradition of Bondoukou, although such patterning is generally widespread particularly in this area of West Africa (as, for example, among the Yoruba). It might be expected that a particular range of warp-stripe patterns is characteristic of a particular group of weavers, and indeed this is probable although as yet unproven for lack of thorough field investigation. Some patterns also include stripes in the weft, i.e. an occasional indigo stripe if the cloth is predominantly white, or vice versa, but these stripes have a 'veiled' effect because of the predominance of the warp, rather than the strength of colour obtained in the warp stripes.

It may be, as Venice Lamb also suggests, that the *khasa*, the Fulani woollen blankets which are imported for specific ceremonial uses, have had some influence on the development of Asante weaving patterns. The *khasa* is, of course, weft-faced and it could perhaps be argued that the characteristic development of Asante weaving beyond simple warp-stripe patterns is in fact the result of attempting to reproduce weft-wise patterning in a warp-faced weave structure.

Some Asante cotton cloths are indeed elaborated by means of the incorporation of small areas of weft-faced weave, called *bankuo*, and also small areas of supplementary weft floats. Both are produced with the *asanan* double-heddle as described above. In the *bankuo* areas of a cloth, the weft-wise bands of solid colour which are woven completely hide any stripes laid in the warp. Just to confuse matters it is, of course, possible to weave warp-wise stripes in weft-faced areas by using alternating weft elements in two colours. Those in the one colour will then all lie over one warp unit and under the next, and vice versa for weft elements in the other colour. For the area

117

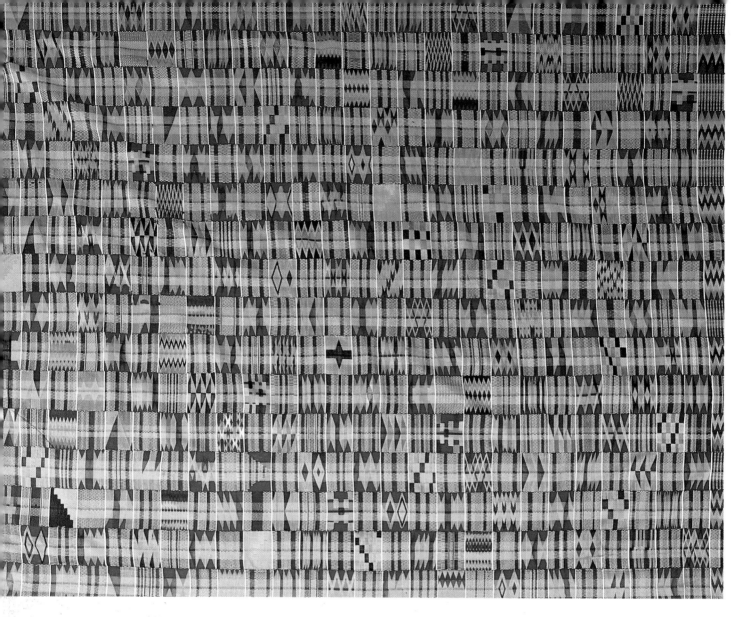

Above Detail of a silk textile, Asante, Ghana. Woven of imported silk yarn with a great variety of supplementary weft-float patterns: a fine example of *adwinasa* ('my skill is exhausted'). Alastair and Venice Lamb Collection, National Museum of African Art, Washington, D.C.

Opposite An Asante chief, Ghana, wearing a silk textile of the so-called 'double weave' variety.

of supplementary weft floats, the *asanan* heddles permit the pattern weft to float alternately over and under one or more units of six warp elements across the pattern area. After each passage of the supplementary weft the ground weft is also laid by means of the *asatia* heddles. This particular technique is described (see Emery, 1966) as overshot for at no point is the extra weft actually laid in with the ground weft (if it were it would be wholly or partially hidden according to the effective predominance of the warp).

It is on the more brightly coloured silk (and now rayon) cloths that these techniques are the most extensive. Cloths described as *adwinasa*, 'fullness of ornament' (Menzel, 1972), usually glossed as 'my skill is exhausted', have the entire warp covered with weft-float patterns between the weft-faced bands. It is possible that imported silk cloths were first unravelled in order to embellish cotton cloths using the *asanan* heddles. Blocks of weft-faced weave when rendered in silk are called *babadua*. However, once the warp also began to be laid using silk then an even greater variety of warp-stripe patterns was possible simply because of the different colours available. Because the cloth is woven in narrow strips and then cut and sewn selvedge to selvedge it is necessary for the weaver to ensure the regular spacing of pattern areas in order to secure their alignment when the strips are sewn together. This he does by means of a measuring stick.

We have already mentioned two levels of Asante weaving: the cotton cloths for general use and cloths partly or wholly of silk for court use. Cutting across these two levels, however, Venice Lamb (1975) tells us that Asante weavers distinguish three categories of woven textile according to the patterns: *ahwepan*, cotton or silk cloths

118

Left Detail of a cotton textile, Asante, Ghana. Woven of indigo and white machine-spun yarn in strips about 4 in (10 cm) wide showing ten different patterns of warp and weft striping. Alastair and Venice Lamb Collection, National Museum of African Art, Washington, D.C.

Right Detail of a cotton textile, Ghana. An example of the 'Liar's Cloth' pattern. Alastair and Venice Lamb Collection, National Museum of African Art, Washington, D.C.

Page 122–3 Detail of a cotton and silk textile, Ewe, Ghana. Woven of machine-spun cotton in strips about 3 in (8 cm) wide with seven different patterns of warp striping alternating with weft-faced stripes, and with areas of supplementary weft-float patterning, in silk. 1934. 3–7. 165; Beving Collection.

with warp stripes but with no additional pattern; *topreko*, 'single weave' cotton or silk cloths with weft-faced areas and extra weft floats; and *faprenu*, 'double weave'. The latter is essentially a further elaboration of the overshot supplementary weft floats in which the extra weft is worked across the pattern area *and back again* between each pick of the ground weft to give areas of solid colour which look as if they are tapestry weave. (They could, of course, be rendered without a ground weft as tapestry weave but they are not.)

There is one additional category of silk cloth over which the King of Asante had a complete monopoly. These are the *asasia* cloths, distinguished by a further elaboration of supplementary weft patterning. Venice Lamb (1975) gives a full account of *asasia* cloths. They are woven using three pairs of heddles, one for the ground weft and two for the supplementary weft floats. The extra pair of heddles permits an overlapping diagonal arrangement of floats characteristic of twill weaves. Each unit of six warp elements after passing through the second pair of heddles is divided so that three elements of one unit combine with three of the unit next to it in order to pass through the third pair of heddles.

In any discussion of the names and categories of Asante cloth the word 'kente' must be mentioned as it has passed into common use as a general term for Asante silk cloths. It is said, however, to be a corruption of the Fante word for basket. The chief of Bonwire told Venice Lamb that it was originally used by Fante traders for the handwoven cloths they purchased in Kumase for resale on the coast. The word is not 'traditional' among Asante weavers. Non-*asasia* silk cloths may be referred to as *ntama*, which simply means 'cloth', or as *nsaduaso*, which implies cloth of a better quality; and there are the categories of 'plain', 'single weave', and 'double weave' referred to above.

Each supplementary weft-float design and each of the different patterns of warp stripes has its own individual name; and the cloth as a whole, when the strips are

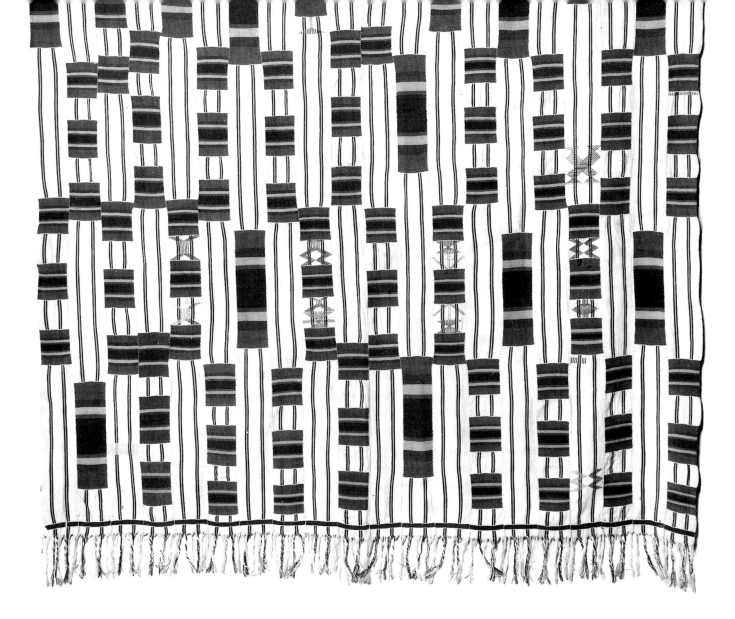

Detail of a cotton textile, Ewe, Ghana. Woven of machine-spun cotton in warp-faced strips 3½ in (9 cm) wide, white with thin indigo and yellow stripes, alternating with blocks of weft-faced striping in red, yellow, blue and green, and with the occasional supplementary weft-float patterning. This cloth was collected by the donor's father in about 1900.
1955. Af 5. 252; Miss M. Best.

sewn together, will be known by the name of the warp-stripe pattern. Some of these pattern names are descriptive of some feature of the pattern itself although for many, if not perhaps most of them, the association of name with pattern appears to be arbitrary. This would seem to be true when a name has some historical significance and also when a pattern is named by a proverb. There may, however, be more subtle and iconic associations: for example, the pattern known as 'Liar's Cloth' in which the distinctive feature is three or four stripes in the warp on an otherwise plain ground. These stripes proceed along one side of the cloth then turn at right angles proceeding weft-wise to the other side, then at right angles again continuing warp-wise, then at right angles back to the other side, etc., creating a meander pattern all the way along the cloth. Brigitte Menzel has illustrated how this is done (1972). 'Liar's Cloth' is said to have been worn by the King of Asante when holding court 'to confute persons of doubtful veracity' (Rattray, 1927). Venice Lamb (1975) discusses at length the significance of pattern names, and Rattray (1927) and Brigitte Menzel (1972) both illustrate large numbers of different patterns with their names. The Rattray series is in the collections of the British Museum.

The elaboration of Asante weaving can be interpreted as a function of the development of the Asante state. Today, by contrast, weavers in Bonwire are hampered by a decline in the quality of yarn available and its increase in price. Moreover the repertoire of patterns together with the technical skill needed has decreased (Lamb, 1975). Although the new, post-colonial élite of Ghana wear these cloths, they appear satisfied with a restricted range of patterns. They neither make the demands nor impose the standards previously expected of an Asante weaver. This

Detail of a cotton textile, probably Ewe, Ghana. Woven of very fine hand-spun cotton in weft-faced strips about 3 in (8 cm) wide, in red, green, yellow, white and blue (the red and green now faded). This cloth is said to have been presented to the vendor's father by the King of Dahomey in about 1865. 1954. Af 1. 1.

cannot therefore ensure the maintenance of the full range of designs evolved during the past two or three centuries, let alone stimulate the invention of new patterns. Asante weavers always wove to order and only the sub-standard and reject cloth found its way to market. Most Ewe weavers, by contrast, have always woven for the market, and as they frequently weave in an Asante manner to a non-discriminating audience this too must be a factor in the decline of Asante weaving.

Ewe weaving: The weaving of the Ewe peoples of south-eastern Ghana has its own independent history and distinctive styles with even greater diversity of pattern than is found among the Asante. Venice Lamb (1975) and Posnansky (1989) give full descriptions of it.

There are four areas of Ewe weaving. The first is among the Anlo in the extreme south where the coastal town of Keta was the principal market, though now the main market has been moved to Agbozume. Anlo weavers employ the same techniques as the Asante using both cotton and silk (and now rayon), but the patterns of warp stripes and supplementary weft floats are quite distinctive to the tutored eye. The weft-float patterns are sometimes representational and resemble those on the Djerma cloth mentioned earlier. Like the Yoruba, but unlike the Asante, Anlo weavers also employ ikat-dyed yarn, and Venice Lamb suggests that the older the Anlo cloth the more Yoruba it seems. Anlo weavers also produce a lower quality of cloth for export to 'the Congo' employing a colour range distinct from that typical of cloth for home consumption. The second centre of Ewe weaving is in the Adangbe area to the north of the Anlo. Here there is little fine weaving at the present day but old cloths are carefully preserved particularly for ceremonial use. The earliest of these are exclusively

125

Silk and cotton hammock, Ewe, Ghana. Woven of a silk warp with weft-faced areas and supplementary weft floats in machine-spun cotton. The plying of yarn of more than one colour for the weft-faced areas together with the figurative float patterns are characteristic of some Ewe weaving. Length 120 in (310 cm). 1981. Af 13. 1.

weft-faced and are similar to the four-inch-web cloths apparently emanating from the Timbuktu area, described above. The Adangbe also weave warp-faced cloths and alternating warp- and weft-faced strips with a pattern of supplementary weft floats. The Adangbe claim to have taught both the Anlo and the Asante how to weave. The third centre of Ewe weaving is around Kpandu. Cloth woven here is characterised by a greater use of hand-spun cotton and simpler patterns of warp stripes and weft floats. Finally, in the Ewe heartland of Notse, Togo, hand-spun indigo-dyed cotton is still woven for local ceremonial use with patterns only of warp stripes.

In all three areas except the last the blocks of weft-faced weaving and the supplementary weft-float patterns are produced, as among the Asante, by means of a second pair of heddles.

Manjaka-Papel weaving: European influence on textile design in West Africa has generally been limited to the effects of imported yarn, dyes and cloth, and has not included direct intervention in the design process. There is, however, the inevitable exception. The Portuguese appear to have included weavers among the slaves taken to the Cape Verde Islands and to have introduced complex geometric patterns, often, perhaps, of Moroccan derivation, into their weaving. The cloths manufactured were traded around the West African coast as well as into Europe. The particular style of weaving which developed subsequently found its way back to the West African mainland where it was taken up by the Manjaka and Papel peoples of Guinea-Bissau. At the present time, Cape Verde weaving is apparently defunct although it continues

A close-up view of the Mende tripod loom in action. The weaver is beating in the weft.

to flourish in Guinea-Bissau and its technical innovations have been copied and developed by adjacent Manding weavers.

The cloths are woven in strips about seven inches wide, in a balanced weave tending towards weft-faced plain weave, using white machine-spun cotton, with complex and extremely dense geometric patterns of supplementary weft floats. Alastair and Venice Lamb have seen the Manjaka loom in operation (1984). The patterns are woven by means of a large number of supplementary heddles operated by an assistant at the weaver's instruction.

Variations of loom structure: The setting up of an Asante loom has been described in some detail and it is, perhaps, now appropriate to describe the variations in the structure of the narrow-strip double-heddle loom throughout West Africa. A great many looms are illustrated in the literature on this subject (for example: Boser-Sarivaxévanis, 1972b and 1975; Lamb, 1975, 1980, 1982, 1984; Menzel, 1972), and we do no more here than summarise some of the points which they have noted. To recapitulate, the double-heddle loom has the following parts: the framework on which the warp and the machinery for weaving it is mounted, which may or may not incorporate breast and warp beams; the dragstone and its sledge; the beater; the heddles together with their suspension above and pedals below; the shed stick; and the shuttle.

The simplest framework of any West African loom is the tripod used by Mende weavers of Sierra Leone. At one end the warp is attached to a cloth beam supported

127

Detail of a cotton textile, Cape Verde Islands or Manjaka, Guinea-Bissau. Woven of machine-spun yarn in strips about 7 in (18 cm) wide, white with complex supplementary weft patterning in black. 1934. 3–7. 195; Beving Collection.

between two posts, and at the other, sometimes to a peg beside which may be a basket containing the rest of the warp, sometimes to another beam supported by two posts. Over the warp is placed a tripod of sticks from which the heddles are suspended. The beater is not suspended from this framework as elsewhere but is held up simply by the warp elements passing through it. The upper part of the beater has an extension to one side to give the weaver a handle with which to manipulate it.

The weaver sits beside the loom to operate the pedals and as weaving progresses the tripod, heddles and beater are moved along from cloth beam to warp post. When the exposed length of warp is woven it is rolled onto the cloth beam and a further length, taken up from the warp in the basket, is exposed. The apparatus is moved back to the cloth beam and weaving continues. Thus the shedding device moves along the warp, rather than the warp being continually pulled through the shedding device; this, of course, is what happens with the fixed single-heddle, 'raised ground' loom, described above, found in North-east Africa, Cameroun, and elsewhere.

Most other double-heddle looms in West Africa are supported on four posts which are usually driven into the ground. Among the Asante and Ewe the framework is carefully carpentered and fixed to a wooden base while among the Yoruba, and sometimes among the Hausa, the frame is replaced by a lean-to shed from the roof of which the apparatus is suspended. Again, among the Hausa, the apparatus may be hung in the branch of a convenient tree. For almost all West African double-heddle looms other than that of the Mende tripod the weaver sits behind the cloth beam.

The dragstone and sledge, by means of which the warp is held under tension on all West African double-heddle looms other than the Mende and the Manjaka and Papel, was described at the beginning of this chapter; together with the narrow web, it is the most idiosyncratic feature of West African weaving.

Everywhere except among the Mende the beater is suspended from above the loom. Again, on all looms other than the Mende, the beater is rectangular in shape, but it differs among the various peoples according to the relative size of the four parts of the frame in which the slats are set. Among the Yoruba all four are roughly of equal size and thickness. Among the Hausa the bottom piece may be deeper, and the whole frame bound in leather. Among other peoples the bottom piece of the frame is very much heavier than the other parts of it, thus increasing the force with which the weft can be beaten in.

In a few areas, including the Mende, the heddles are suspended from a rocker or horse, a rod suspended at its centre, to each end of which is tied one of the heddles. Occasionally the heddles are joined together by a leather strap which passes over a rod either tied to the top of the loom frame or, as in the case of the Fulani of the inland Niger delta region of Mali, suspended between a pair of enormous flat wooden objects carved in the shape of the letter J (if one stands to the left of the weaver). Renée Boser-Sarivaxévanis gives the Fulani name for this device as *tonngi*; and it is suspended from the loom framework. By far the most widespread method of suspending the heddles is by means of a pulley which may be hooked over part of the loom frame, as among the Ewe, or suspended from it, as among almost all peoples other than those mentioned in this paragraph. The pulley may be relatively large, as among the weavers of Senegal and also the Fulani (who employ the pulley as well as the *tonngi*), but it is usually quite a small object. It is often carved, particularly among the peoples of Ivory Coast. The heddles themselves seem to show little variation of form except according to the width of the cloth woven with them.

Renée Boser-Sarivaxévanis (1975) describes how the Fulani *tonngi* heddle suspension device is associated with a pair of extremely long pedals. These are constructed in such a way that they take the weight of the entire legs of the weaver, who must sit at this loom with his legs fully extended in front of him. These features are apparently explained by Fulani weavers as adapted to the nature of woollen yarn and the difficulties of shedding it (the reason, perhaps, why both they and the Berber women weavers of Kabylie have now generally switched to using cotton for the warp). She suggests that the Fulani, or their ancestors, were the first to possess the double-heddle loom in West Africa as they alone would have had yarn capable of being woven. With the domestication of cotton, however, they were, because of their appreciation of the 'internal logic' of weaving, able to adapt their equipment to suit the new material; and this, Renée Boser-Sarivaxévanis suggests, happened in two stages. The first consisted of replacing the *tonngi* with a pulley, but still retaining the long pedals; and in this form the loom spread to the Tukulor, Serer and Wolof peoples of Senegal. The second stage consisted of replacing long pedals with short pedals operated by the feet instead of the whole leg; a cotton warp is easier to shed than a woollen one. In this form the loom spread throughout the rest of West Africa. Among Asante, Ewe and occasionally Yoruba weavers the short pedals are replaced by calabash discs which are gripped by the weaver's toes. The mechanical principle, however, is the same. The Fulani weavers of Mali possess all three types of loom although the intermediate stage (pulley with long pedals) is obsolete. There is, of course, no obvious reason why this sequence could not have proceeded the other way round. Indeed, some weavers in that area (Hoffman, 1987) assert that cotton has greater antiquity than wool.

Renée Boser-Sarivaxévanis does not comment on the Mende loom, however, which others see, in view of its several aberrant parts, as a possible prototype loom with the single-heddle raised ground loom as its fore-runner. Another hypothesis proposes a link with the 'pit' looms of North-east Africa. We have no wish to comment upon or adjudicate beween the different hypotheses regarding the origin of the double-heddle loom in West Africa. We have taken Renée Boser-Sarivaxévanis' scheme principally as a useful way of explaining some of the mechanical differences between looms. It is, after all, not essential that there must be only one point of origin or source of inspiration.

Finally, having considered all the other parts of the double-heddle loom, we come to the shed stick and the shuttle. The former is often just a short flat piece of wood, though among the Asante shed sticks with a head carved at one end have been known. Among the Yoruba weavers of Ilorin, it will be remembered, the shed stick was used in association with one or more supplementary single-heddles to make the extra weft-float patterns. The shuttle is usually a boat-shaped object in which the bobbin carrying the weft yarn revolves. There are, of course, minor variations of shape and size and in many areas the weft proceeds out through an eye in the side of the shuttle boat. Among the Asante the sides of the shuttle are cut away. Mende weavers do not use a shuttle of this form at all but wind yarn around a stick of suitable length. In principle this shuttle is similar to that used by Nigerian women with the single-heddle loom.

Heddle pulleys. *Left to right*: from the Baule of Ivory Coast, the Dogon of Mali and the Guro, also of Ivory Coast, 1956. Af 27. 38, 4, 25, Mrs Webster Plass; another from the Baule, 1944. Af 4. 186, Mrs Beasley; and from the Asante, Ghana, 1950. Af 32. 1. Height of tallest 9½ in (24 cm).

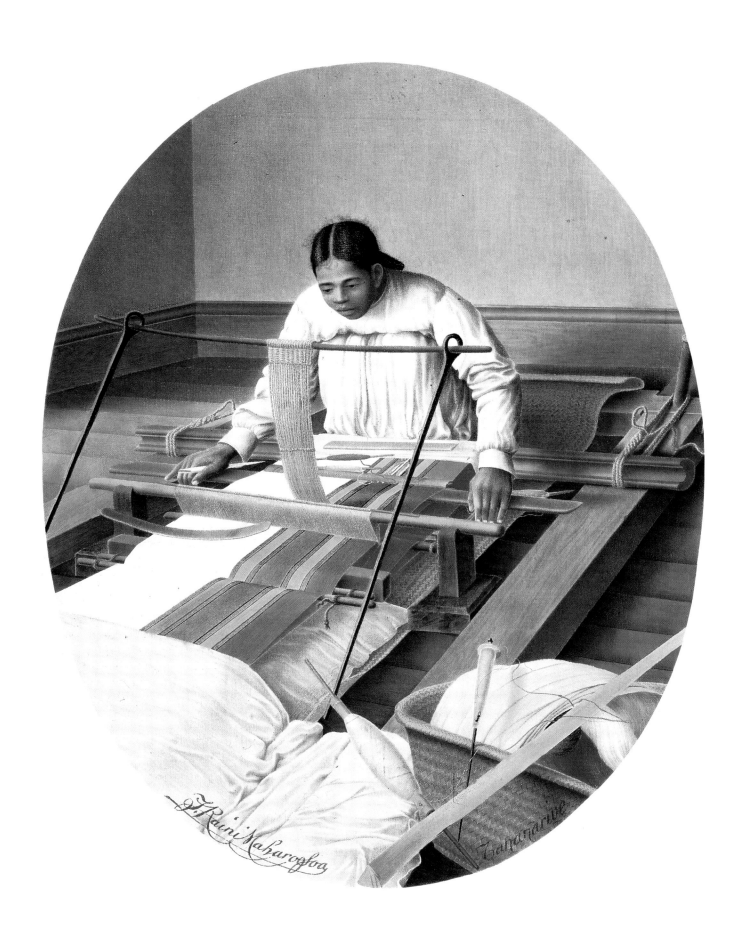

CHAPTER SIX

WEAVING

IN

MADAGASCAR

A Merina weaver, Madagascar, as portrayed in a painting dating from the early 20th century. The loom with its supplementary single-heddle shown suspended above the warp system is used for weaving complex bands of pattern in the weft.

In earlier chapters occasional reference has been made to textile production in Madagascar, and it will perhaps already be clear that in their weaving practice, as in almost all aspects of their culture, the Malagasy peoples are distinctive within the context of Africa. Some features of their diverse weaving technologies are found only on the island and nowhere else in Africa, while others which have a localised distribution on the continent are none the less known to the Malagasy. Silk, cotton, raphia (itself a word derived from *rofia*, the Malagasy term), bast, banana fibre and in more recent times wool are all used either alone or in combination on one of the several loom types found on the island. Such variety makes it convenient to summarise the main features of Malagasy weaving in a separate chapter.

Behind the diversity of such weaving practice, as in the island's material culture in general, lies the unique range of cultural influences assembled in Madagascar in the 1,500 or so years since it first began to be settled. A review of the archaeological and historical evidence is provided in Mack, 1986. Briefly, Malagasy, the language spoken with dialect differences throughout the island, is classed as Malayo-Polynesian. Kiswahili is hardly spoken at all even as a second or trading language, and in general the number of terms in Malagasy itself that are of Bantu and thus African origin is minimal. This affirms most strikingly the South-east Asian origin of much in Malagasy culture, though it does not, of course, mean that African influences are absent. In addition, Madagascar attracted considerable numbers of Arab settlers especially as the long-distance trading links of the East African coastal region developed at the beginning of the present millennium. Among European influences, British missionaries sought to improve on indigenous technologies in the nineteenth century, in particular by introducing new methods of spinning, while the French colonial administration through the establishment of Ateliers des Arts Appliqués tried to expand on and market traditional arts. This diverse cultural background accounts for much of the variety of Malagasy weaving, although the identity of individual groups of settlers may not have been retained into modern times.

Loom types

Single-heddle looms: Reports of Malagasy weaving have tended to identify a type of fixed heddle horizontal loom with the island; references to any other forms of loom to be found in Madagascar are rare. The loom in question is in principle the same as that found until the recent past in Eastern and Southern Africa (as illustrated on p. 57 above and in the photographs reproduced in Davison and Harries, 1980). The loom is

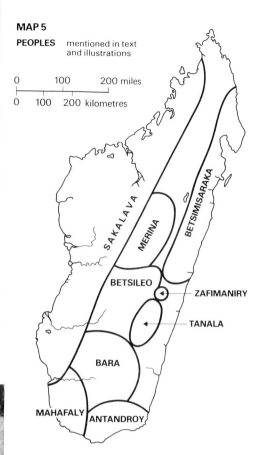

MAP 5

PEOPLES mentioned in text
and illustrations

0   100   200 miles

0   100   200 kilometres

The island of Madagascar.

Top left Betsimisaraka loom for weaving
raphia cloth, as set up inside a hut,
Madagascar. The heddle is firmly lashed to
the rafters by cords and remains stationary
throughout the weaving process. The shed
stick pulled close to the heddle and turned
on its side brings the shed to the weaver's
side of the heddle and allows the weft to be
drawn through using the weaving sword.

Centre left For the next pass of the weft the
shed stick is pushed back, away from the
weaver, thus creating the reversal on the
weaver's side of the heddle. Pressing down
with a loose stick helps open up the gap so
the weaving sword can be negotiated
through.

Bottom left The weft is beaten in with the
weaving sword.

furnished with a single-heddle. However, double-heddle looms are also found in
Madagascar, and there is variation in the methods used to create tension in the warp.
A version of the draw loom also occurs amongst the Merina. This refinement is
discussed in the section on Malagasy cloth below.

When we were working on the first edition of this book we assumed that the term
fixed heddle did not apply in the strictest sense to the majority of Malagasy looms.
Linton (1933) describes a Tanala loom on which the heddle is placed on supports to
separate the warp elements and form the first shed. Once the shuttle has been passed
through and the weft beaten in, the heddle rod is simply slipped off the supports and
the countershed is formed. It is replaced on its supports to form the next shed and so
on. This, in effect, is a similar method to that adopted on Saharan ground looms.

In the light of our own subsequent field observations, however, it is now clear to us
that the loom described by Linton is the exception and not the rule (indeed, we have
reasons to doubt the accuracy of his account). Virtually all Malagasy single-heddle
looms employ a method of suspending the heddle throughout the process of weaving.
It is not by manipulating the heddle that shed and countershed are effected but, as in
the vertically-mounted Berber loom (as illustrated on p. 60), by manipulating the shed
sticks. In the Malagasy case, of course, the loom is laid out horizontally, but otherwise
our discussion of the operation of the Berber loom could almost suffice as a description
of its Malagasy counterpart. The loom is also comparable to ones photographed in the
Yemen (Weir, 1975, plate 4) and to some South-east Asian looms.

As set up, the heddle, placed securely on its supports, acts to raise one set of warp
elements above the other and fixes their position which is retained throughout the
weaving process. The cross-over point lies down the loom from the weaver and on the
far side of the heddle, its position determined by the insertion of a shed stick. The
shuttle is passed through the shed thus created and beaten in with a wooden weaving
sword. To create the countershed the shed stick is pulled backwards in the direction of
the weaver until it is adjacent to the heddle itself. Owing to the thickness of the shed
stick the cross-over point now passes just beyond the heddle on the weaver's side, and
pressing down on the warp with a loose stick assists in opening up the gaps. By
passing the weaving sword through and turning it on its side this can be further
opened up to permit the next pick of the weft. Although it is perfectly feasible for one
woman to complete all these operations alone, among the Betsileo it is usual for up to
four women to work together.

The heddle itself may be supported in one of several ways. The usual practice is to
attach it to pegs, whether driven into the ground or free-standing. Which method is
adopted seems largely to depend on whether or not the heddle needs to be moved
along the cloth as the cloth is woven. In weaving on looms with a continuous warp
there are two main possibilities. As the warp is wound continuously round two beams
the result is a warp system in which the elements run in two parallel planes. In the
case of the horizontal loom from Sudan discussed on p. 56 above, and for that matter
on the Berber vertical loom, both of these planes are woven together, and the resulting
cloth is of the same approximate length as the distance between the two beams of the
loom. Here it is necessary to move the heddle along the warp as weaving proceeds. A
similar practice occurs in Madagascar, the clearest example being from the Mahafaly in
the south-west of the island (Molet, 1956). The looms from this area employ free-
standing supports so they can readily be moved together with the heddle as
necessary.

The second alternative is to weave on only one plane of the continuous warp, as is
the practice on the Nigerian woman's loom (p. 67). In this case one of the loom's
beams is loosened periodically during the process of weaving and the already woven
cloth is pulled round bringing a further length of unwoven warp onto the plane on
which weaving is taking place. In other words, it is the warp which is moved as
weaving proceeds, and the heddle remains more or less in position. Within this type
of weaving there is no particular advantage in having mobile heddle supports, and in
many parts of Madagascar these are often driven into the ground and remain in
position throughout. An alternative is to lash the heddle to the rafters of a hut, as is

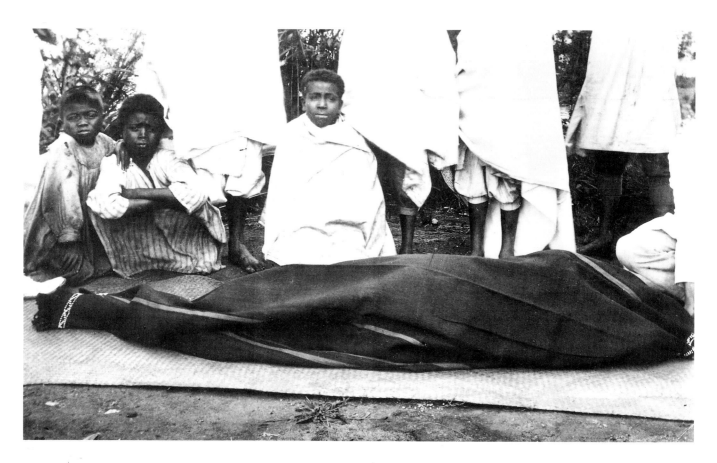

Mourners, wearing appropriate white shawls (*lamba*), crouch beside a corpse wrapped in a 'colourful' shroud (*lamba mena*).

used at this point. The usual procedure is to lay the warp ready for mounting on the loom. The warp elements are then divided up as required into bands according to the desired pattern of warp striping, and those which are to be dyed a particular colour are separated off from the rest. These are wrapped up tightly in raphia leaves or some other material that will resist the dye. On being submerged in the dye, therefore, only the exposed bands will take the colour. The same procedure is followed for other bands that are to be dyed in different colours, with the already dyed sections being included in the part that is wrapped up.

Warp 'ikat' dyeing was also practised until recent times. This was the speciality of some Sakalava groups in western Madagascar (in particular of weavers at the villages of Kandreho, Ambatomainty and Sitampiky). The tradition appears to have died out within the last few decades (Heurtebize and Rakotoarisoa, 1974). The warp was dyed at intervals along its length giving patterns which can work horizontally or vertically. Figurative designs, mostly of people, were also occasionally produced by these means. Such cloths always seem to have been woven of raphia and were used for purposes as diverse as mosquito nets and burial shrouds. The technique is rarely found in Africa and then only in a few parts of West Africa. The presence of such methods in Madagascar should rather be regarded as a reflection of the island's wider Indian Ocean context.

In general, the design of Malagasy textiles is characteristically carried in the warp, even if, as in the case of ikat, the pattern can work across rather than exclusively along the cloth. There is, however, one major exception. This is the tradition documented for the nineteenth century and perpetuated until contemporary times of weaving highly elaborate geometric motifs across the width of the textile using weft floats. The practice appears to have been limited to the Merina, and it is only Merina weavers who practise this technique at the present time. In the past such weft patterning characterised the colourful textiles worn by noble families; nowadays it is largely restricted to the white silk *lamba*.

We once assumed that such elaboration could have been produced only by the introduction of some form of industrialised process. Malagasy looms appeared to lack the technical means with which readily to effect such patterning; and most in fact are without the sophistication required. Our subsequent fieldwork, however, has revealed that amongst the Merina the patterns are produced by the use of one or more supplementary single-heddles arranged in sequence across the warps. Each supplementary heddle is used to produce one band of pattern and each need be little more than 15 cm in width. If they are arranged in sequence across the loom, the gaps between are occupied by blocks of warp striping on coloured cloths or plain white and unpatterned on contemporary textiles.

Weavers sit at their looms with bits of paper beside them. These are little more than rows of numbers but they are vital to the process for here have been counted off and recorded those leashes that need to be manipulated on the supplementary heddles to establish the succession of sheds that yields particular patterns. Even the most complex of designs can be accurately recreated by these means. The most prolific of professional weavers in Imerina usually have sheafs of such papers that allow a large

Detail of an ikat-dyed raphia textile, Sakalava, Madagascar.

Above Detail of a cotton textile, Betsileo, Madagascar. The border is here decorated with small white metal beads which have been clipped onto the warp and then woven in as the weft is applied. Width 69 in (177 cm). 1928–58; Field Museum.

Left Detail of a silk textile, Merina, Madagascar. The float weave patterns are distinctive of 19th-century cloth reserved for aristocratic use. The blue/green background suggests that this example was woven for royalty, these being royal colours. 1988. Af 12. 1.

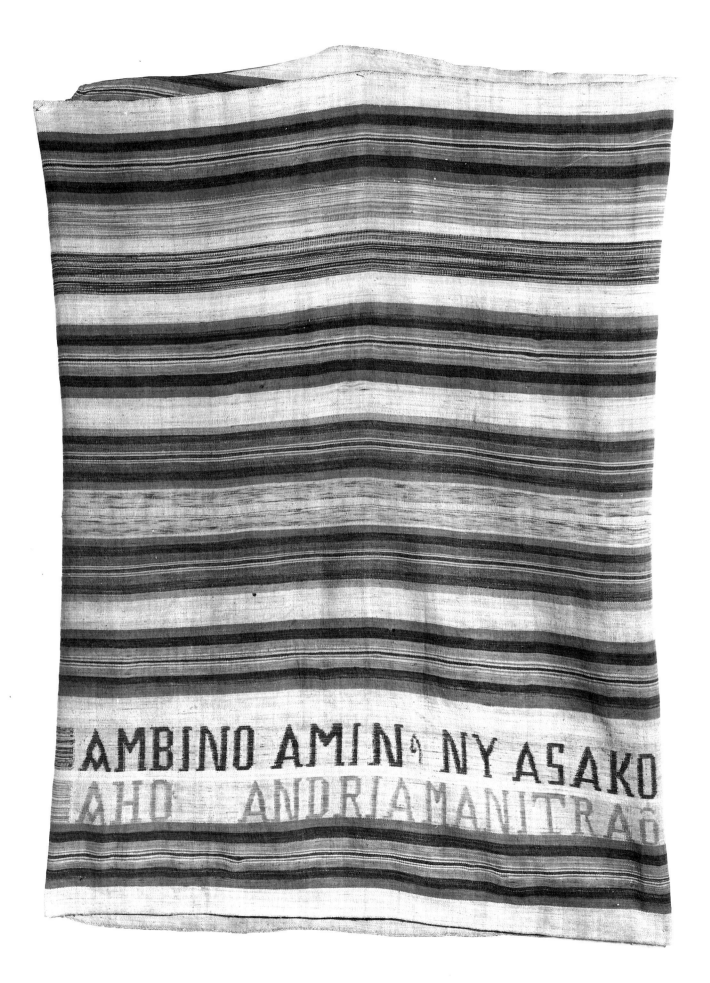

range of designs to be effected. The patterns have been passed from one weaver to another, though one woman with whom we discussed the matter said she had copied many of hers from the walls of the Royal Palace in the capital and worked out for herself how to reproduce them.

Finally, we should mention another means by which weft patterning is applied to cloth in Madagascar. This is by the creation of pattern along the borders of the cloth at either end of the warp. Several methods are used, but the oldest seems to be a form of appliqué in which small cylindrical beads of tin, lead, or, some authorities suggest, silver are clipped round the warp threads once the textile has been woven. Most of the patterns thus created are geometric, and the technique is characteristic of some Betsileo textiles and those of the Antandroy and Mahafaly to their south. Occasional figurative imagery – the most familiar of which are designs of humped cattle – is also found. The textiles thus produced might according to size and shape be used either as burial shrouds, shawls or loincloths.

Nowadays other means are also adopted to create these patterns. One is the introduction of white or sometimes of coloured weft in the course of weaving to give a band of patterning along the borders. The other incorporates small holed glass or plastic beads. We assume that these must be arranged on the warp as the loom is set up and simply woven in with the weft.

Woman's raphia skirt, Betsimisaraka, Madagascar. Woven on the single-heddle loom, an inscription has been created in the border using supplementary weft floats. In translation it reads: 'Bless me in my work, O God, that I may prosper.' Width 29 in (74 cm). 1984. Af 14. 152.

CHAPTER SEVEN

PATTERN

DYEING

Detail of a resist-dyed raphia textile, Manyema, Zaire. The central area of this cloth has been dyed yellow using the brimstone tree. The tie-dyed panels to each side have been dyed in 'camwood'. Width 42 in (107 cm). 1954. Af 23. Q; Wellcome Collection.

Dyes must be counted among the raw materials of textile manufacture: obviously, if colour is to be introduced to the weave structure of a cloth the yarn must be dyed before it is woven and we have, therefore, already surveyed the dyes found in Africa and some of the processes of dyeing, particularly of indigo which is by far the most popular. We have also described the simple patterns of colour variation Yoruba, Hausa and Ewe dyers introduce by tie-dyeing warp yarn before it is mounted on a loom: the method generally known by the term 'ikat'. The Baule of Ivory Coast, but especially some Sakalava in Madagascar, make particularly complex ikat patterns.

We now turn to the use of dyes upon cloth subsequent to its manufacture on the loom. In practice, of course, both hand-woven and factory-made cotton fabrics are dyed. The dye used at this stage, as also for ikat-dyeing, is almost exclusively indigo. Exceptions to this rule include the following: in parts of Sierra Leone and Mali hand-spun cotton is sometimes dyed brown; in Senegal kola nuts are occasionally used to give an orange-brown effect; the Bamana of Mali employ yellow and black but then discharge the yellow dye; the Kuba of Zaire make use of a different range of dyes to produce various shades of yellow, orange, red, black and purple. Otherwise, apart from indigo the entire range of dye colours available seems to have been used only in the preparation of yarn *before* weaving. The subject of dyeing in Africa, and particularly of indigo-dyeing, is a complex one. In an attempt to provide a comprehensive account of textile design in Africa no more than a brief summary can be attempted here.

One of the most famous and important centres of indigo-dyeing in West Africa is the Hausa city of Kano in northern Nigeria. In the mid-nineteenth century it was estimated that there were some two thousand dye pits in use there; and yet Kano dyers specialise mainly in dyeing plain white cloth with no pattern added by any of the methods of resist-dyeing to be described below. Resist-dyeing is not unknown among Hausa dyers but it is generally regarded as a relatively recent imitation of Yoruba methods. One particular speciality of Hausa dyers is the manufacture of extraordinarily shiny indigo-dyed cloth for turbans, which capitalises on the way in which the cloth, heavily overloaded with dye, can be beaten to give a shiny, burnished effect. These turban cloths are highly prized not only among the Hausa but throughout the southern fringes of the Sahara, especially by the Tuareg; and their prestige value seems to enable them to command a price far higher than one might expect from the materials and labour involved in their production. It should perhaps be noted that among the Hausa the dyers are men in contrast to the Yoruba and the Soninke (or Sarakole) whose dyers are women.

Right Resist-dyed woollen textile, Ayt Atta, Morocco. This woman's headscarf has been first dyed yellow and then tie-dyed black. 18 in (46 cm) square. 1969. Af 37.2.

Above A Hausa boy taking tie-dyed cloth out of a dye pit in Kano, Nigeria.

Resist-dyeing in one or more methods is found in most of the regions of textile manufacture in Africa. Frequently a cloth is tied or stitched tightly in some way so that the tying or stitching prevents the dye penetrating the fabric and, when unpicked, leaves pale areas on a dark ground. Alternatively, some starchy substance can be applied to the textile. This too will resist the dye giving pale areas on a dark ground when washed off at the end of the dyeing process.

Probably the commonest method of tie-dyeing is the formation of patterns of large and small circles in various combinations. This is found particularly among the peoples of Senegal and Gambia, the Yoruba of Nigeria and more generally throughout West Africa. For the larger circles the binding thread is wound tightly around a bunched-up area of cloth and tied securely. If, instead of pulling the cloth into a bunch it is carefully folded before tying, the shape which results will be more rectangular in form. For the smaller circles, the binding thread is used to tie in a seed or a small stone. Some Kuba raphia cloths are dyed in this way and a plaited raphia garment from south-west Ivory Coast in the collections of the British Museum is tie-dyed in two colours. Berber women of Morocco sometimes tie-dye patterns of rectangles on a headscarf. These shapes are called 'mirrors' and held to be prophylactic against the evil eye; but not all patterns necessarily imply this kind of meaning. Patterns of circles on a Yoruba cloth might be called 'big moons and little moons', 'moons and stars', or 'moons and fruits', but these are descriptive of the pattern rather than indicating some other level of meaning.

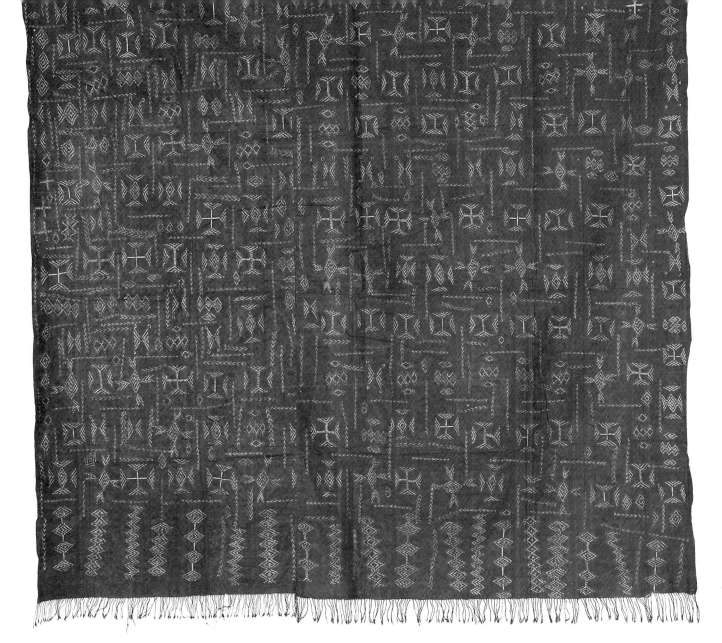

Above Resist-dyed cotton textile, Senegal. This cloth, an imported cotton fabric, has been embroidered before dyeing. The stitching resists the dye. The fringe has been made by unravelling the weft and plaiting the loose warp ends thus exposed. Width 55 in (140 cm). 1934. 3–7. 244; Beving Collection.

Right Resist-dyed raphia textile, Kuba, Zaire. Strips of cane stitched to the cloth are used to resist the dye. Width of guilloche pattern 5 in (13 cm). 1908. Ty 426.

Above Detail of a resist-dyed cotton textile, Gambia. The 'marbled' effect is produced by carefully crumpling the cloth before dyeing. It will be loosely bound together for immersion in the dye pot. The fabric used is woven of hand-spun yarn in narrow strips on the man's double-heddle loom. Width 41 in (104 cm). 2796.

Right Detail of a resist-dyed cotton textile, Abakwariga, Nigeria. An example of the so-called Cameroun cloths produced by the Abakwariga, the Jukunized Hausa craftsmen of the Wukari area. The cotton fabric is stitched with raphia before dyeing. This cloth has been burnished to bring out the sheen made possible by excess indigo on the surface of the fabric. Width 85 in (212.5 cm). WA 11.

Far right Detail of a resist-dyed cotton textile, Igbo, Nigeria. A cloth stitch-dyed in northern Igboland for use by the Leopard Society of the Cross River area of south-eastern Nigeria. Width 69 in (175 cm).

Another method of tie-dyeing found in Senegal, Gambia and Sierra Leone consists of folding a strip of cloth into several narrow pleats and binding them together. The folds and the binding resist the dye to produce a cross-hatched effect. Senegalese dyers also crumple cloths up into loose balls and tie them up into a package to dye them. After dyeing an irregular blotched or marbled effect is created. This may be carried out twice, first with the orange-brown kola nut dye and second with indigo.

In addition to tying and crumpling, a cloth may be stitched; and there are at least three ways of 'stitch-dyeing'. Some Kuba cloths have had strips of cane stitched along them to make simple interlacing and striped patterns. When removed, the cane is found to have resisted the dye. The Yoruba employ a technique of folding cloth and stitching the folds, and both Yoruba and Senegalese dyers sew a simple running stitch along a cloth and then draw the whole cloth together in a series of small folds. Senegalese dyers also embroider geometric patterns on cloth. When the cloth is dyed and the embroidery unpicked very finely-executed designs emerge. A similar technique, though carried out on a much larger scale by stitching strips of raphia fibre over the surface of hand-spun cotton cloth, is employed in the grasslands of the Cameroun (Lamb, 1982) and by the Abakwariga of the Wukari area of north-eastern Nigeria. (The Abakwariga are a Jukunised Hausa people who supply the Jukun with their material culture.) Perhaps the most striking of all stitch-dyed fabrics are the *ukara* cloths illustrated and described by Keith Nicklin (1977, plate 25). They are displayed at meetings and ceremonies of Ekpe, the Leopard Society of the Ejagham and Efik and other people of the Cross River area of Nigeria, and are covered with Ekpe motifs. They are made to order in northern Igboland.

Finally, also in Senegal, rice paste may be applied to a cloth. Methods include the rice paste being splattered on at random, or applied over most of the cloth and patterned by running a comb through it.

Yoruba *adire* cloth

The Yoruba word for indigo resist-dyed cloths is *adire*. The centres of the art are Abeokuta and Ibadan, though some dyeing is done throughout most of Yorubaland. Factory-made white cotton shirting is the fabric used and two lengths each about two and a half yards long and a yard wide are prepared. When the dyeing is complete these will be sewn together and hemmed to give a more or less square cloth. In relatively remote rural areas in and around Yorubaland one could, in the 1960s, still see women wearing resist-dyed hand-spun cotton cloths (usually as a way of renewing an old cloth) with very simple patterns made by sewing sticks and stones into a cloth before dyeing.

There are two broad categories of *adire*. In one the resisting agent is raphia, *iko*, and patterns are made by tying and stitching. These cloths are called *adire oniko*. In the other category the resisting agent is starch, *eko*, which is either painted or stencilled onto the cloth before dyeing. These are called *adire eleko*. Nancy Stanfield gives a full account of all the processes by which these cloths are dyed in her contribution to *Adire Cloth in Nigeria* (1971).

In preparing *adire oniko* two or more thicknesses of cloth are placed one upon the other and tied together. Patterns of large and small circles as described above are very common. There are several standard combinations each with its own name, for example: a series of small circles tied in a spiral is called *alekete*, 'caps', three very large circles each with a ring of small circles around it is called *osubamba*, 'full moon'; five rows of large circles with the intervening area filled with small circles is called *olosupa-eleso*, 'moons and fruits', etc. Another method of tie-dyeing consists of folding two thicknesses of cloth in narrow pleats to form a bundle which can be tied together. The binding and to some extent the folds resist the dye and the pattern which results can have the shape of lines, chevrons, or a series of rectangles of increasing size depending on the alignment of the folds.

Adire oniko on which the patterns are stitched are known as *alabere* (*abere*, needle). Again, raphia is used, this time with a needle. Two cloths are usually sewn at once and are folded into tucks or pleats before stitching. The stitches have to be pulled very tight

A Yoruba woman tying the folded cloth, preparatory to dyeing.

Yoruba *adire* cloth, Nigeria. Tie-dyed cotton
shirting. Width 65 in (165 cm).
1971. Af 35. 4.

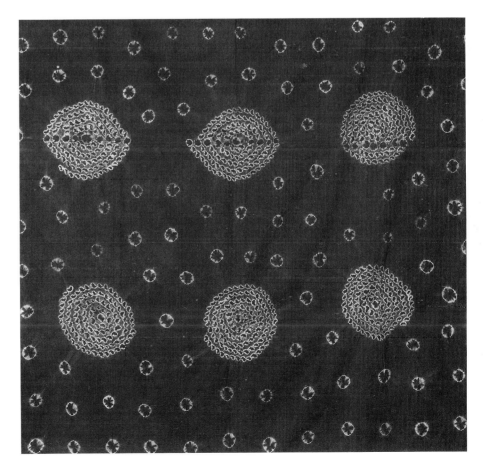

Detail of a Yoruba *adire* cloth. Nigeria.
Folded and tied before dyeing. As in all
adire cloths two pieces have been dyed and
then sewn together edge to edge.
Width 58 in (147.5 cm). 1971. Af 35. 11.

153

Detail of a Yoruba *adire* cloth, Nigeria.
Stitched and dyed, with small tied circles, a
pattern called 'plantain' or 'the lazy man
cannot be proud'. Length 68 in (173 cm).
1953. Af 17.10.

Painting starch onto a cloth before dyeing
it, Yoruba, Nigeria.

Cutting a stencil at Abeokuta, Yoruba, Nigeria.

Above A collection of stencils photographed at Abeokuta.

Right Detail of an *adire* cloth, Yoruba, Nigeria. Painted freehand with starch before dyeing in indigo in order to resist the dye. This combination of designs is called *Ibadandun*, 'Ibadan is a happy place'. The pillars of Ibadan town hall, alternating with spoons, can be seen at the bottom right, second square up. The cloth is prepared in two identical halves which are then sewn together. Width 71 in (180 cm). 1971. Af 35. 15.

to resist the dye. A cloth with squares filled with cross-hatching is called 'cocoa'; a series of stitched columns with chevrons is called 'plantain'; a very common pattern called *agosofin* consists of stitched squares which are alternately filled with stitched lines and tied circles; a pattern incorporating a stitched eight-pointed star is called 'fingers'. A series of columns drawn together by running stitches makes a pattern called 'threepences are scattered all around the house'. Where a running stitch is used it will be used to draw the cloth together before it is dyed. After dyeing, when the cloth is dry the stitches can be cut but the raphia is never pulled out completely so that the purchaser knows that the cloth is newly-done. A form of *alabere* is now made by men using sewing machines. Two cloths are folded and stitched. A common pattern of criss-crossing lines is called 'eggs'.

Adire eleko are resist-dyed with starch made from cassava flour. In some places yam flour may also be included. The flour is mixed with water, boiled and strained to remove any lumps. A small piece of copper sulphate, which can be purchased in most markets, is added when the starch is boiling to make it last longer. On the free-hand painted cloths a bunch of chicken feathers is used together with the very thin midrib of a palm leaf (taken from a household broom) for the finest lines, and a matchstick or something similar for making spots. Starch is applied thickly and on one face only. The painter must take care that she does not crack the starch. When the painting is complete the cloth is very carefully hung over a bamboo pole to dry. It is important that the starch be properly dry before the cloth is dyed. The principal centre for the free-hand painting of cloths is Ibadan. For all the other methods, Abeokuta is the main centre of manufacture.

Starch can also be applied to a cloth through a stencil and, as with machine-stitching, the cutting of the stencil and the application of the starch through it is men's work. The stencils are cut from sheets of thin corrugated roofing sheet which have been hammered flat, though the linings of tea chests are said once to have been used. Designs are measured and marked on the metal, which is cut with a chisel. The size of these stencils varies considerably. Nancy Stanfield suggests that an average size is twelve inches by eight inches. To apply the starch, the cloth is spread out on a table, the stencil placed in position on it, and starch applied by means of a semi-circular piece of pliable metal. The stencil is lifted and replaced on another part of the cloth. If

Yoruba *adire* cloth, Nigeria. Painted freehand with starch before dyeing. This combination of designs is called *Olokun*, 'Goddess of the Sea'. Width 69 in (175 cm). 1971. Af 35. 17.

several stencils are used on one cloth the most important is used first all over the cloth, then the next, and so on until the pattern is complete. The starch must then be allowed to dry as with the free-hand painted cloths. Once the cloth has been duly immersed in the dye and has thoroughly dried the starch can be removed. The cloth is hung over a pole and soaked with buckets of cold water, and the wet starch scraped off. As starch is applied only to one face of the cloth, the dye is only resisted on that face. The other will be indigo all over. The cloth is then finished by beating it with wooden mallets over a piece of smooth wood to render it smooth and shiny. With repeated washing both the texture of the cloth and the colour of the dye soften as starch and indigo are gradually washed out.

The free-hand painted cloths are usually divided into rectangles within each of which particular geometric or representational patterns are drawn. There are a fairly restricted number of named configurations of these patterns. Jane Barbour (1970) provides an extensive catalogue of *adire* patterns and illustrates twenty-eight of these painted cloths of which nineteen belong to one or other of eight standard configurations. Of the remainder, three are variations upon one of the standard sets, while four others are simple repetitions of one or two of the patterns from one of the eight standard sets.

One of these is called *Ibadandun*, 'Ibadan is a happy place'. Each half of the cloth (the two halves are prepared separately and then sewn together) has four rows each with seven rectangles, a total of twenty-eight. Jane Barbour illustrates seven examples of *Ibadandun* and no two are alike. They differ in the style of the hand which has painted them, the degree of care given to their execution, and in the range of patterns included in the rectangles. The range of patterns is standard for a cloth bearing the name *Ibadandun* but on some the number of repeated patterns in the twenty-eight squares is greater than on others. One pattern which always appears two or three times is composed of the pillars of Mapo Hall alternated with spoons. Mapo Hall is a neo-classical style building on a hill in the middle of Ibadan, which serves as a town hall. It was built around 1945 by the famous Taffy Jones, himself a pillar of public building and works in western Nigeria. In other rectangles the patterns are composed of such

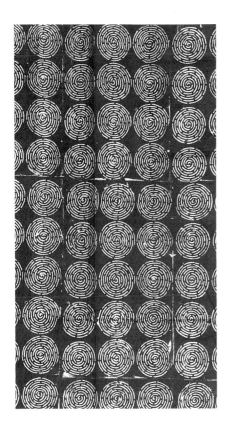

Above Detail of a Yoruba *adire* cloth, Nigeria. Here again the starch has been applied through a metal stencil before dyeing. This pattern is called 'Spinning Tops'. 1953. Af 17. 20.

diverse objects as frogs, watches, scorpions, roundabouts, eggs, paralysed legs, ducks, the leaves used in chieftaincy initiation rites, umbrellas, snakes, chameleons, mirrors, forks, Koran boards, guinea fowl, sugar lumps, and so on.

Another popular configuration of patterns is called *Olokun*, the goddess of the sea and of wealth. Each half of this cloth is composed of two rows each of five squares, with a row of small rectangles around the perimeter of the cloth. Cloths bearing this name again differ as to the style of the individual hand and the care exercised in the painting but the content of the ten large squares on each half is constant. Many of the patterns are geometric, although some portray such varied subjects as chicken wire, matches, crocodiles, birds, scorpions, fish, spinning tops, scissors, four-legged stools, and chieftaincy leaves. Some of these elements overlap with *Ibadandun* but the patterns in which they are incorporated do not.

A third free-hand cloth described by Jane Barbour is called *Sunbebe*, a name apparently of erotic significance which refers to the beads a woman wears under her clothing and which should only be seen by her husband. Each of the twenty-eight rectangles into which the two halves of this cloth is divided is filled with very finely painted geometric patterns in a style analogous to the stitched patterns described above. Some of the geometric forms depict motorcar tyres, snakes, leaves, a king's horse-tail fly switch, etc.

Stencilled cloth patterns probably present the greatest variety of all. The patterns include many geometric and representational forms and among the latter are elephants, spinning tops, keys, skyscrapers, chicken wire, matches, birds, the tree whose leaves are used for chieftaincy initiation rites, toads, 'OK' and divination boards. Jane Barbour illustrates a fair selection of these, too.

Perhaps the most curious of all the stencilled cloths are those called *Oloba* (literally, 'owner of a king', i.e. the cloth with a king on it). In the centre of each half of this cloth

Right Detail of a Yoruba *adire* cloth, Nigeria. Painted freehand with starch before dyeing, though copied from a stencilled design. The inscription at the bottom is, however, stencilled. It reads: *gbogbo ohun kosehin oluwa*, 'everything is known to the Lord'. The figures in the central medallion are King George V and Queen Mary and are doubtless copied from Jubilee souvenirs of 1935. On each side can be seen the winged horse upon which Muhammad flew from Mecca to Jerusalem, together with many other figures and motifs. 1971. Af 35. 24.

Above Two Yoruba women beating cloth after dyeing to smooth and burnish it.

Opposite Yoruba *adire* cloth on sale in an Ibadan street.

is an oval medallion over which are the remains of letters evidently cut by a craftsman who did not fully understand which bits of each letter were significant in distinguishing one from another. The ultimate sense of the lettering is, in fact, 'King George and Queen Mary'; and the design is evidently copied from the Jubilee souvenirs of 1935. However, among the motifs to each side of the royal couple can be clearly discerned the image of a fantastic horse derived from a popular Muslim devotional picture printed in Cairo, which could be purchased in almost any Nigerian market. It is *Al-Buraq*, the horse upon which the prophet Muhammad flew from Mecca to Jerusalem in his dreams. It has a woman's head wearing a crown, wings, and a peacock's tail. These features together with the assorted birds and minarets which provide the background to the picture can all be discerned in the Yoruba stencilled version to each side of the King and Queen together with other motifs including lions, elephants and many others of uncertain interpretation. Below the design a stencilled inscription: *gbogbo ohun kosehin oluwa*, 'everything is known to the Lord', is usual, although *olowo ju ologun lo*, 'a rich man is more [powerful] than a medicine man', sometimes occurs.

These stencilled designs run through several variations and also several stages of decadence in the copying of the original patterns. Sometimes lions completely replace Muhammad's horse, or Adam and Eve replace King George and Queen Mary (and the particular representation of the primordial couple which appears is drawn from another popular Muslim devotional picture also printed in Cairo). The *Oloba* or 'Jubilee' in the collection of the British Museum is in fact a free-hand painted copy of

'Discharge-dyed' cotton textile, Bamana, Mali. The ground fabric is woven of hand-spun cotton yarn in narrow strips on the man's double-heddle loom. It has been first dyed yellow and the design applied with river mud which 'saddens' the yellow, turning it dark brown. The yellow dye in the unpainted areas has then been discharged with a caustic preparation returning the fabric in those areas more or less to its original natural colour.
Width 34 in (86 cm). 1956. Af 27. 10; Mrs Webster Plass.

the original stencilled design. A selection of cloths showing these developments is illustrated by George Jackson (1971).

Bamana mud cloth

Finally, one last and aberrant method of dyeing must be mentioned. This is the *bokolanfini* (or *bogolanfini*) cloth of the Bamana described by Imperato and Shamir (1970) and Brett-Smith (1982). Narrow-strip cloth made of hand-spun yarn is first washed with water and dried in the sun. It is then dyed yellow with an infusion prepared from the leaves of *Anogeissus leiocarpus* and *Combretum glutinosum*. Mud from a dried-up pond which had been collected a year previously is applied to one side of the cloth according to the desired pattern. It is allowed to dry and then dipped in water to wash off the mud. The cloth is immersed in the yellow dye again and given another application of mud. The design appears yellow on a dark ground. The yellow, however, is now removed. Peanuts, caustic soda, millet bran and water are mixed together and heated. This preparation is then carefully painted over the yellow design and the yellow turns brown. The cloth is dried in the sun for a week and the 'soda soap' is washed off leaving the design white on a dark ground. (John Donne (1973), discusses the chemistry of this curious process.) These cloths, together with cloths simply dyed yellow or brown, are worn as tunics by hunters and other men.

CHAPTER EIGHT

DRAWN, PAINTED, PRINTED AND STENCILLED PATTERNS

Detail of a large sheet of European cotton shirting with drawn and painted magical designs of Islamic inspiration, collected amongst the Asante, Ghana. (The individual rectangles are about 7 in (18 cm) in width.) 1951. Af 3. 1; Mrs Stevens.

In all of these decorative techniques liquid is applied to a cloth in some way other than the various methods of dyeing described above.

Drawing and painting

The art of drawing and painting on rock surfaces in Africa has been minutely analysed and the comparable practice of drawing on or engraving calabashes is also fairly well documented. Relative to this, however, the techniques of drawing and painting on cloth is little recorded and very few examples have been collected. The only definite evidence of its existence as a decorative technique is in Zaire (see, for example, Margaret Trowell (1960), plate XXVI), among the Hausa of northern Nigeria, the Ibibio of south-east Nigeria, in the grasslands of Cameroun and among the Senufo of Ivory Coast. Two examples from Ghana in the British Museum's collections were probably the work of itinerant Hausa craftsmen rather than a local product. One reason for this rather scant distribution may be the difficulty of applying paint without it running along the planes created by the interweaving of elements in the textile. Additionally, of course, the colours will fade quickly in the sun unless the pigment is of an appropriate composition. As with dyes, the substances applied must be mordant.

Amongst the Hausa the art of drawing appears to have developed in association with the conversion to Islam in the southern Saharan region. Certainly, as with the appliquéd flags of the area (see below), the technique has been used in transcribing Koranic texts onto cloth. A speciality of the Hausa seems to have been the production of charm gowns for the protection of the wearer against evils which might befall him. David Heathcote (1974b) describes one such gown which, in 1971, he commissioned to be made for him, having previously seen the example in the British Museum. The results provided important documentation of the tradition. To render the gown an effective prophylactic instrument three elements seemed to be necessary. First charms were attached to the garment itself, these being Koranic texts written out on paper and encased in a leather pouch. Secondly, the garment was soaked in water which had previously been used to wash Koranic writing boards. The final stage was the inscription of Koranic characters on the cloth itself, a greater number on the back than the front because the back was considered the more vulnerable area. However, the Koranic script that was applied to the cloth was rather muddled. It seems that calligraphic skill and Koranic scholarship are not consistently met together in one person. Drawing on cloth seems to have been the work of draughtsmen otherwise employed in laying out the designs to be embroidered on cloth, in divining and

Cotton tunic, probably from northern Nigeria. The drawn inscriptions are derived from Koranic texts. Small leather charm cases, which probably also contain extracts from the Koran, are attached to the inside of the garment. Length 35 in (89 cm). 1940. Af 23. 1; Captain A. W. F. Fuller.

making amulets, rather than a sideline for men of learning. Certainly this was so in 1971.

In addition to the charm gown in the collections of the British Museum there is also a large piece of factory-made white cotton cloth, apparently collected in Ghana, covered with drawn and painted designs. The cloth is laid out in squares which contain geometric patterns in black, red, green and yellow, with every area of unpainted white cloth filled with inscriptions in Arabic. This cloth was probably made by a Hausa man at the behest of some wealthy client as a protective charm.

The painted cloths produced by the Senufo have a protective purpose similar to those of the Hausa. The cloth used is the local cloth woven on the narrow-strip loom, and the motifs are those associated with the Poro men's society: turtles, crocodiles, snakes and masked figures being amongst the most frequent images found. The painted cloths are used by Poro initiates as ceremonial dress and also by hunters. The traditional method of applying the designs was to lay out the required patterns with a greenish paint made from boiled leaves. A solution made from mud was then carefully applied using the edge of a wooden or metal knife and the design thereby outlined in a darker colour. These technqiues still survive in the Ivory Coast, though in recent years cloths of this kind have been produced for sale to tourists in the local markets. Commercial drawing ink has begun to replace the traditional vegetable dyes, and the various motifs are no longer arranged on the cloths in the traditional manner.

Two other examples of a painted cloth have been noted. One is in the Pitt Rivers Museum, Oxford, and is clearly the work of the Annang-Ibibio of south-eastern Nigeria. The style of painting is that otherwise found in their funerary shrines. The other is a cotton tunic recently acquired by the British Museum from the grasslands of Cameroun which has painted designs on it that seem like a negative version of the stitch-dyed cloths described in the last chapter.

Printing

There appear to be very few cases of designs being printed on cloth in Africa. One is that of the well-known *adinkra* cloths of the Asante, first discussed in detail by Rattray (1927). The 'canvas' for these stamped designs is either a plain white cotton cloth or a cotton cloth dyed brown, red, green, purple or blue. The technique itself is traditional and the original fabrics to which the designs were applied would have been locally-woven cloth produced from hand-spun cotton. Now, however, the designs are usually found on imported cloths which in a society with a strong and surviving tradition of textile production provides a means of assimilating cheap externally-produced cloth to local circumstances. The earliest example of *adinkra* cloth in the British Museum's collections was collected in 1817 by T. E. Bowdich.

The pigment which is used for decorating the cloth is prepared from a tree bark. This is boiled up for several hours in a solution which includes lumps of iron slag, and a thick black liquid is produced which Rattray describes as having something of the consistency of coal tar. The stamps themselves are made from pieces of old calabash cut to different designs, and a small handle is made from sticks which are pegged into the back of the calabash pieces. To apply the designs the cloth is laid out on a dry flat piece of ground which has been swept clean, and it is held taut with wooden pins. The next stage is to divide up the cloth into squares which is done by drawing directly onto the cloth with the thick black dye, often using a comb. The designs are then printed in each of the squares on the cloth.

The designs themselves are not arbitrarily chosen. Rattray lists fifty-three different motifs and he considered this a more or less complete series. Each had an appropriate

Adinkra stamps, with examples of printed cotton cloth. Asante, Ghana. Stamps: 1946. Af 18. 237-243; D. H. F. Wilson. Esq. Cloths: 1934. 10–22. 22–25; Captain R. P. Wild.

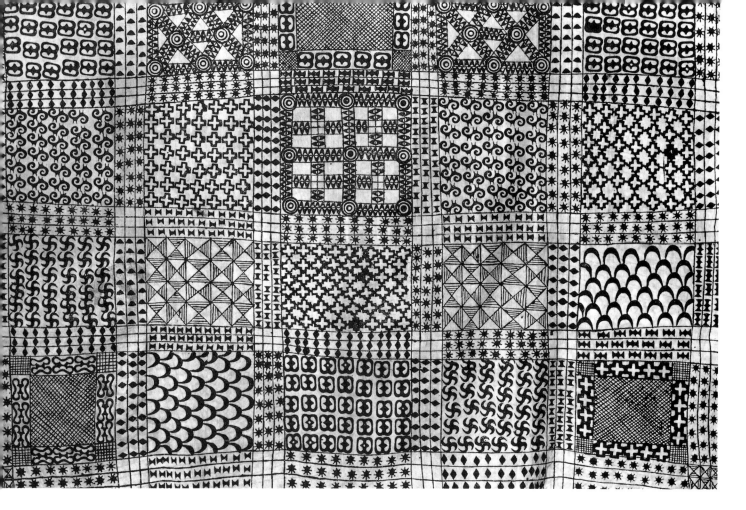

Detail of an *adinkra* cloth, Asante, Ghana. W A 22; T. E. Bowdich, who collected it in 1817.

name and most of these have historical, allegorical or magical significance. To give just one example analysed by Rattray himself: a design with a central circle and spokes leading outwards from its circumference bears the name *Se die fofoo pe, ne ce gyinanturi abo bedie*, which Rattray translates as 'What the yellow flowered *fofoo* plant wants is that the *gyinanturi* seeds should turn black'. This, he explains, refers to a particular plant with a small yellow flower which on dropping its petals turns into a black, spiky seed. It is the latter which is represented in the design, but the pattern name has a further allegorical meaning for this is a saying which refers to a jealous person. Associations such as these seem to be particular to the Asante vocabulary of pattern.

A second instance of printed designs occurs along the Swahili coast of Kenya and on the off-shore island of Zanzibar, where printed cotton cloths, or *khanga*, were formerly produced. Printing blocks were used which were both larger than their Asante counterparts, and incorporated more than one motif per block. The blocks themselves appear to have been locally manufactured sometime around the turn of the century, and have the designs cut into the wood. Sometimes nails, bits of iron, or wooden pins are added to the design to produce particular patterns. However, Mrs Jean Brown (to whom we are grateful for bringing details of this example to our attention), suggests that the idea of stamping or printing was probably not indigenous but was copied from Indian prototypes.

Stencilling

The main examples of designs being stencilled onto cloth occur in West Africa and these have already been covered in the section dealing with Yoruba *adire* cloths. One other African case, however, is known. Amongst the Ganda stencilled designs on barkcloth are sometimes encountered. The designs are non-representational and are produced from a stencil cut from the banana leaf. The dye is black and is made from a mixture of marsh mud and vegetable matter. However, the whole process of manufacture is shrouded in secrecy. Bruce Kent, to whom we owe this little information, was unable to discover more about the process or the possible meanings of the designs in spite of successive attempts.

Above Adinkra cloth being made in Kumase, the Asante capital.

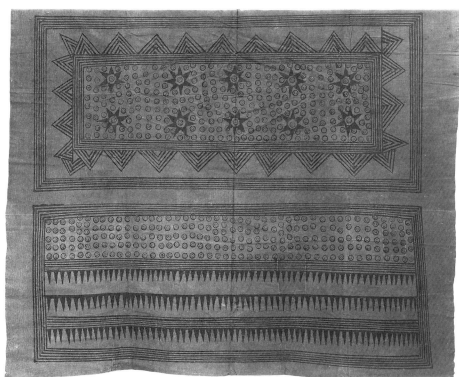

Right Stencilled barkcloth, Ganda, Uganda. The cloth is reddish brown in colour with patterns stencilled on it in black. Width 80 in (202 cm). 1930. 5–17. 16; H. J. Braunholtz, Esq.

167

CHAPTER NINE

APPLIQUE AND RELATED TECHNIQUES

Strips of metal are here applied to red flannel over a basketry base with feathers around the circumference. The mask around which this object is placed is made of netted fibre and is worn by a masquerader performing at an Akoko-Edo age-grade ceremony, Nigeria.

Appliqué is the word used to describe the process of adding further materials to an already-woven textile base. Normally the term is applied to the laying on of additional pieces of textile, but we also here include such supplementary materials as beads and shells, metals and jewellery, animal fur and bundles of medicine. Taken in this broad sense, the technique can be seen to be well established throughout Africa: ceremonial cloth, banners and flags are often appliquéd; so too are cloths incorporating magical substances and the skins with beadwork decoration of eastern and southern Africa. The technique is certainly indigenous in Africa. It would appear that precisely because appliquéd cloths have a particular distinction, by comparison with undecorated textiles, their owners or wearers would frequently acquire such cloth to mark their own distinction and identity. Where appliquéd cloth is found in Africa, as often as not it is associated with prestige and social position.

A good illustration is provided by the banners and flags which at one time proliferated in some parts of the continent. These flags were for the most part used in military contexts and many were appliquéd though some were made up by patchwork and a few were embroidered. Those of the Fante of Ghana, for instance, were used to distinguish the different *Asafo* military companies, and the same might possibly have applied to those used by their northern neighbours the Asante. However, the best-documented of the West African banners are produced by the Fon people of Dahomey, now the Republic of Benin. Herskovits (1938) tells us that all appliqué work was done for the Fon by a restricted guild in Abomey and their work included ceremonial cloth caps, hammocks, and state umbrellas, as well as flags and banners. The members of this cloth-working guild were, in the main, retained to work on commission for the chiefs and nobles, and the cloths they produced often incorporated designs and motifs specifically requested by their clients. Thus a man who had been successful in military campaigns might commission a banner recording his exploits, and many flags had just such a narrative form. The narrative was built up by showing a sequence of figures whose successive actions followed those of the incidents being related. Other cloths, however, included images associated with particular people or classes of people. The king, for instance, might commission flags and cloths including images of the lion, the white-breasted crow, the shark or the harp – all representations associated with royalty. Many of the images themselves seem to be derived from the patterns found in bas-relief on the walls of palaces.

The cloth-workers always kept the patterns from which the textile fragments to be appliquéd were cut. A man's descendants, therefore, could commission new flags or

169

170

Left Cotton appliqué banner, Fon, Republic of Benin. Length 69 in (177 cm). 1982. Af 23. 1.

Right Silk appliqué flag, Fante, Ghana. Length 43 in (135 cm). 1978. Af 22. 1.

Below Appliqué waist cloth, Asante, Ghana. The design, here executed in imported fabrics, is said to be the invention of Anokye, the 18th-century Asante priest. Width 11½ in (29 cm). 1935. 11–4. 8; Captain R. P. Wild.

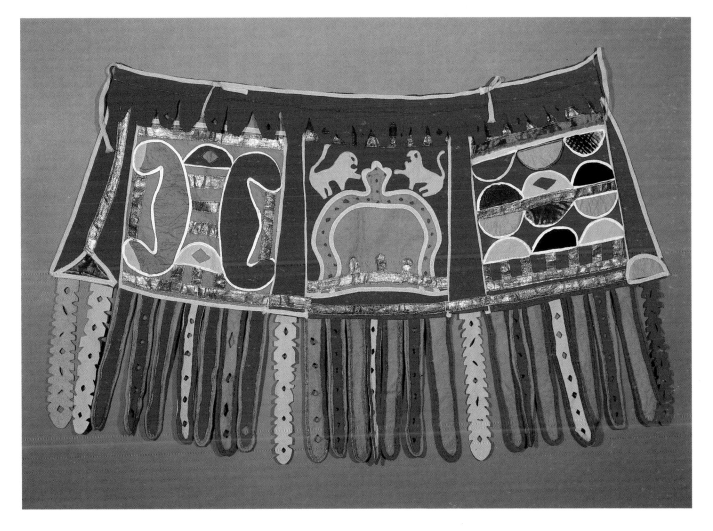

banners which included an arrangement of images that had become associated with his family. In this way appliquéd cloths became heraldic devices, prestige images associated historically with particular families. Among the appliquéd cloths in the British Museum is an Asante waist cloth, the patterns of which are said to have been designed by Anokye, a priest who is associated with the founding of the Asante nation at the beginning of the eighteenth century.

The background of the cloth itself was plain and the appliquéd images were in a naturalistic, though sometimes exaggerated, style. The colours of these supplementary pieces were vivid reds, blacks, greens, purples and yellows. On the finished cloth these appliquéd pieces lie flat in spite of the fact that some are relatively large. This may be attributed to the method by which they are attached to the cloth. A pattern is first cut out on muslin or thick paper to the required form. This is then tacked onto the coloured cloth so that the piece to be appliquéd can be cut to the shape. This in turn is then tacked onto the background cloth which is kept flat whilst the appliquéd pieces are sewn in position, the practice being to sew away from oneself not, as elsewhere, towards the body. Appliquéd banners are still made in Dahomey but are nowadays produced for a commercial market and the style and technique have in consequence become debased.

Another place in Africa where flags and banners were once found is in the Sudan, from whence a distinctive appliquéd uniform, the *jibbeh*, also comes. Most of the cloths of this type which have subsequently come to Europe were collected during the various skirmishes and battles in the period from the 1880s until the final routing of the followers of the Mahdi on the field of Omdurman in 1898. As it is the ideology of the Mahdist cult which provides the context within which the wearing of these various appliquéd cloths must be sought, some brief review of this history will be helpful.

A group of men photographed in an Akoko-Edo village in the course of ceremonies which mark the transference of their age-set up to the next grade. Their leader wears a cloth appliqué skirt.

Cotton flag, Sudan. An Arabic text has been cut out of coloured cotton cloth and applied to a cotton ground. Flags such as these were used by the forces of the Mahdi. The text reads: 'O God, the Compassionate, the Merciful, the Living, the Eternal, the Almighty. There is no god but God and Muhammad is the Messenger of God. Muhammad-al-Mahdi is the successor of the Messenger of God'. Width 74 in (188 cm). 1953. Af 22.1; Mrs Boyd.

In 1881, in the region of Kordofan, Muhammad Ahmed, a Dongolese, proclaimed himself the promised Mahdi, or prophet of Islam. He preached a doctrine of universal equality and communal ownership of goods and instilled in his followers a fanatical attachment to the pursuit of an austere and faithful life. The counterpoint to this ideal was the corruption and venality of the Egyptians who by the mid nineteenth century had established authority over the Sudan. It was against Egyptian rule that the Mahdi first announced an intention to pursue a Holy War. By 1883 the Mahdist forces were in control of Kordofan and Sennar and the Mahdist cult was beginning to draw support from many parts of the Sudan. General Gordon was sent by the British Government to arrange the withdrawal of the threatened Egyptian population in the Sudan, but in 1884 he himself was cut off in Khartoum by the surrounding Mahdist forces and in 1885 Khartoum fell and Gordon was killed. The Mahdi was now on the point of destroying the last vestiges of Egyptian rule, but at this fateful moment he too died. This, however, did not signal the demise of the Mahdist movement for he was succeeded by his main supporter the Khalifa who continued to hold the support of the fanatical Mahdist following. The Mahdist movement succumbed in 1898 with the battle of Omdurman and the defeat of the Khalifa, but still survives as a potent political force in the Sudan.

A number of appliquéd flags survive from this period of Sudanese history. Records of the time indicate that there were two types of flag in use by the Mahdist forces. One was a distinctive green flag which announced the presence of the Mahdi himself, and the other, used by his Emirs, was a plain cotton banner appliquéd with Koranic scripts. Examples of this latter type are still in existence and the texts which they contain consist in the main of invocations to God, a reminder of the religious sources of the Mahdist movement and the conception of the Mahdist mission as that of waging a *jihad*, or Holy War.

The Mahdist movement was but one manifestation of a current of Islamic religious fervour across the region to the south of the Sahara during the nineteenth century. An earlier manifestation of the same movement was provided in the central Sudan, i.e. northern Nigeria and adjacent regions, in the person of Usman dan Fodio. He, together with his sons and followers, declared a *jihad* but in this case against the Muslim Hausa emirates because of their lax ways. Their paraphernalia also included appliquéd flags, of which the British Museum possesses one example.

The term by which the Mahdi described his initial followers was 'dervishes', which is best rendered as 'religious mendicants'. Their dress was the *jibbeh*, a tattered cotton garment roughly patched with large coloured rectangular or square pieces of cloth, a dilapidated form of attire which translated the life of poverty and austerity lying at the heart of the Mahdist ideology into a striking visual image. One example of this garment survives in the British Museum collections. In spite of its unprepossessing character it is an important object because all the other examples of Mahdist clothing which still survive have a much more distinguished nature which belies the conceptual sources of the garment. These latter cloths have appliquéd rectilinear sections of coloured cloth and an appliquéd motif as a top left-hand pocket. Garments such as these were in fact worn by the leaders of the different sections of the Mahdist forces to distinguish them from the rank and file of the following, but the appliquéd sections were clearly derived from the tattered patches on the ordinary Mahdist costume, which may well have been intentional. Without some form of leadership other than that issuing from the Mahdi himself the dervish forces would have been a mere anarchic horde, and less effective in the battle they were waging. There was in fact a very definite structure of authority within the organisation of the Mahdist forces. The retention in officers' tunics of this reference to the patching on tattered garments may be interpreted as an attempt to resolve in costume the ambiguities of leadership in a movement ostensibly based upon an ideal of universal equality. Thus, if these cloths conform to the observation that, by and large, appliquéd cloths tend to have been prestige garments, they so do in spite of indications in the tunics themselves specifically intended to suggest the contrary.

The *jibbeh* are important for several reasons. They certainly bring into sharp focus what we might call the politics of costume, but they also raise an interesting stylistic point. In some circumstances, and the *jibbeh* provides a good example, it is clear that appliqué may be no more than a case of making a virtue of necessity, of turning the need to patch a torn garment with other fabric into a decorative embellishment which is applied whether or not a hole has appeared in the base textile. Appliqué as a form of stylistic conceit, or perhaps deceit, is also found in other parts of Africa. Amongst the Kuba of Zaire, for instance, long appliquéd cloth is made which women wind round their waists to form a voluminous skirt. The applied textiles are usually rectilinear in shape though smaller circular pieces and pieces having a shape rather like that of a comma often appear. The comma shape is found on carved wooden surfaces and in body cicatrisation as well as appliquéd cloth, and it bears the pattern name *shina mboa* (i.e. the tail of a dog). It is thus a thoroughly stylised form and has entered the wider vocabulary of pattern. However, when one looks at the reverse side of many of these cloths it is found that appliquéd sections, and particularly the smaller ones, conceal a hole which has appeared in the garment. The circular pieces of appliqué are particularly interesting. The predominant structure of Kuba design is one of interlocking shapes, and in consequence there is virtually no precedent, certainly none in woven or embroidered cloth, for the circular form. Appliquéd cloth is just about the only surface on which it appears. The conclusion that it is found there because it derives from the need to repair holes in the garment is inescapable. (On more recent cloths the design possibilities of these textiles have been extended by the addition of a

Cotton *jibbeh*, Sudan. The tunic of an officer in the Mahdist army. The applied sections of cloth are probably derived from the tattered patches on the ordinary garments worn by the followers of the Mahdi. Length 33 in (84 cm). 1909. 3–15. 3; Lady Gatacre.

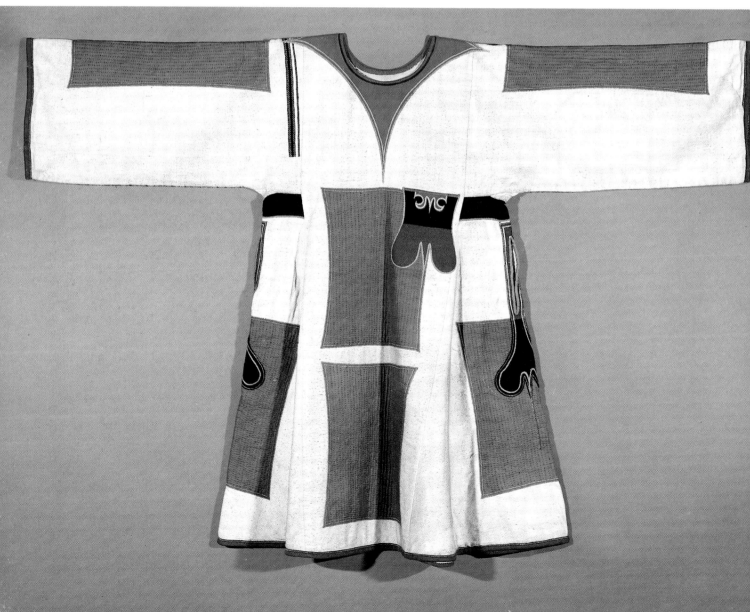

mass of further motifs. These are outlined in black embroidery stitches suggesting appliqué when in fact there is often none (Mack, 1988).)

The theme of imitation, which is also central to the interpretation we have offered of the *jibbeh*, is again a feature of appliqué work which is not uncommon outside the Sudan. Another good example is found amongst the Igbo of southern Nigeria. The Igbo have a series of masquerade performances in which figures appear which are said to have come from the world of the dead. John Boston, who has documented these performances among a group of clans in the north-west of Igboland, remarks that he could find no evidence that any given masquerade was intended to represent any particular ancestor. However, generalised references to character types emanating from the world of the dead did seem to play a part in the iconography of masquerade costumes. One such is the *agbogho mmanwu* or 'maiden spirit' masquerade in which a masked figure portraying the female dead appears. The whole of this particular masquerade costume is conceived in terms of an idealised view of feminine beauty. Boston describes the costume and its visual references as follows:

'The traditional head-dress for female masks is well known in Europe for the fine carving of its thin, angular features and for its elaborate crest carved to represent a traditional hairstyle. Today in all four clans cloth is replacing wood in these head-dresses and the modern article is a cane structure with tassels, bells and mirrors and to which is attached a face of felt embroidered with coloured wools. The costume worn

Above A Kuba woman wearing an appliqué dance costume with substantial areas of design outlined in embroidery stitching, Zaire.

Right Cotton *jibbeh*, Sudan. Roughly patched with brown and blue cloth, garments such as these were the ordinary wear of the followers of the Mahdi. Their ragged condition was a deliberate expression of the life of austerity these 'dervishes' sought to lead. Length 35 in (189 cm). 1886. 6 -28. 1; H. J. W. Barrow, Esq.

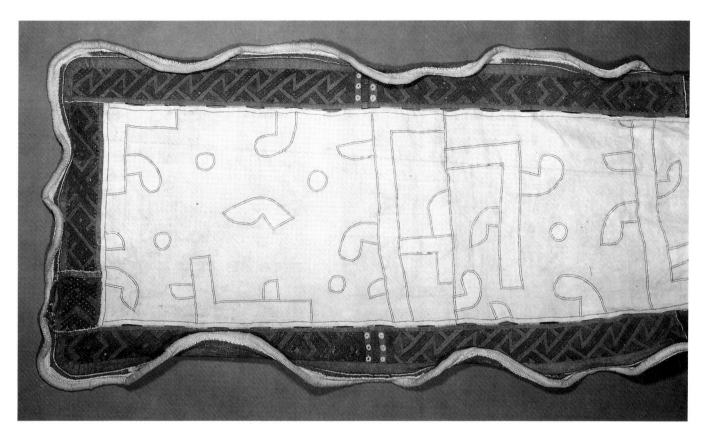

Detail of a raphia appliqué textile with an embroidered border, Kuba, Zaire. A woman's dance costume with the comma-shaped motif called *shina mboa*, 'the tail of a dog'. The edge of the garment encloses a twisted reed producing the wavy edge. Width 24 in (61 cm). 1947. Af 11.1.

by these masks is a two-piece suit of black cloth, decorated liberally with bold designs in vivid colours which represent a masculine interpretation in felt and coloured wool, of body designs which are traditionally a female ornament' (J. S. Boston (1960), p. 60).

In other words this imitation of female body decoration transforms the cloth suit of the masquerade into a symbolic vehicle. Traditionally it complemented the mask and rendered the whole symbolically and visually consistent. Boston observes that in parts of Igboland a skilled tailoring craft has begun to develop to supply such masquerade costumes. For an account of similar masks among the Etsako, one of the groups of Northern Edo peoples across the Niger to the west, see Borgatti (1976). Also among the Igbo groups described by Boston cloth appliqué is used for a gigantic mask known as *Ijele*, a name qualified by such titles as 'elephant' (it is upwards of ten feet tall), 'the great mask and spirit' (it bears representations of, among other things, all the principal masks of the area), 'expensive' (it can only be afforded and therefore commissioned by the more prosperous Igbo communities) and 'beautiful'. For an account of the range of meanings see Aniakor (1978).

This by no means exhausts the instances of cloth appliqué that occur in Africa. The Anang-Ibibio of south-eastern Nigeria, for example, erect commemorative shrines during the obituary rites of the prominent dead. If the particular individual was a man, a chief and a member of the major secret association the shrine consists of a tall screen of bamboo poles and mats in which a large patchwork and appliqué cloth is hung (Nicklin 1977). Among the costumes of the King of Benin at important ceremonial events are cloths with appliquéd figures of leopards and kings.

Visually striking appliquéd cloths from Egypt are known, including an enormous hanging with geometric pattern and Arabic inscription used to line the inside of a tent, an Ethiopian Christian priest's cloak in velvet ornamented with silver and chiefs' capes of lion-skin and velvet. From West Africa there are pagan charm gowns, which parallel the Muslim version described in the previous chapter, but instead of Koranic verses there are animal claws and magical medicines; and there are no doubt other examples.

However, in these cases a deeper appreciation of the relevant traditions and symbolism of appliqué work would be required before an adequate commentary could be provided.

The same, unfortunately, remains substantially true of bead and shell, particularly cowrie shell, appliqué. Throughout West, East and Southern Africa the objects, robes, hats or crowns, and other regalia of chiefs and kings are frequently decorated with these, often so lavishly as to obscure the original textile or other base to which they are applied. The Yoruba, for instance, made tall conical kings' crowns of fine trade beads with faces picked out by the use of different coloured beads. The Yoruba tradition was

Agbogho mmanwu masked figures wearing appliqué costumes, north-western Igbo, Nigeria.

Right The King of Benin in ceremonial dress wearing a skirt of red cloth with appliqué figures of kings and leopards in yellow and black.

Above A wool and hide ceremonial tunic, Benin, Nigeria. Imported red flannel has been applied over a rawhide base and small brass bells attached. Tunics such as this can be seen in brass plaques of the 16th and 17th centuries where they are being worn at the Benin court. The present example probably dates from the 19th century. Length 24 in (61 cm). 1897. 520.

Opposite A shrine set up in memory of a deceased chief among the Anang-Ibibio, south-eastern Nigeria, displaying an appliqué and patchwork cloth made entirely of imported cotton materials.

an eclectic one and crowns imitating the fez or even European royal regalia were also produced. By contrast the Kuba kings (*nyimi*) had caps with a distinctive rectangular peak such as are featured on their portrait statues. These caps or crowns were covered with cowrie shells and beads sewn onto a covering of raphia cloth, and chiefs were distinguished by small conical hats, again lavishly covered with beads and with the feathers of different species of bird attached. The bead and shell designs found on royal regalia no doubt had symbolic significance, though in most cases this has not been recorded and is now lost, other, perhaps, than in the more obvious cases such as the beadwork masks of the Cameroun grasslands. These are the so-called elephant masks, furnished with large flapping circular discs of beads to represent ears and a long bead apron at the front to portray the trunk. The elephant, of course, is a frequent metaphor of kingly power.

In East and Southern Africa beadwork aprons and skirts were widely distributed amongst all social classes, though here again chiefly regalia was often distinctive. It is not unusual to find that each different age-grade has its own beadwork costume or that women who are unmarried or who have yet to produce children wear distinctive bead-appliquéd attire. A man's social development may be charted in many cases according to the different bead costumes he has worn. Similarly a woman's marital status may be announced by the type of beadwork she wears, e.g. two Maasai skirts in the British Museum of animal skin covered with red ochre and decorated with distinctive beadwork patterns are the appropriate attire for an unmarried girl. The

Above Cotton tent hanging with applied
embellishment of Islamic inspiration
in blue, red, white, and black,
Egypt. Width 135 in (343 cm).
1939. Af 9. 33; Mrs H. Perrin.

Left Two Yoruba kings wearing
beadwork appliqué costumes.

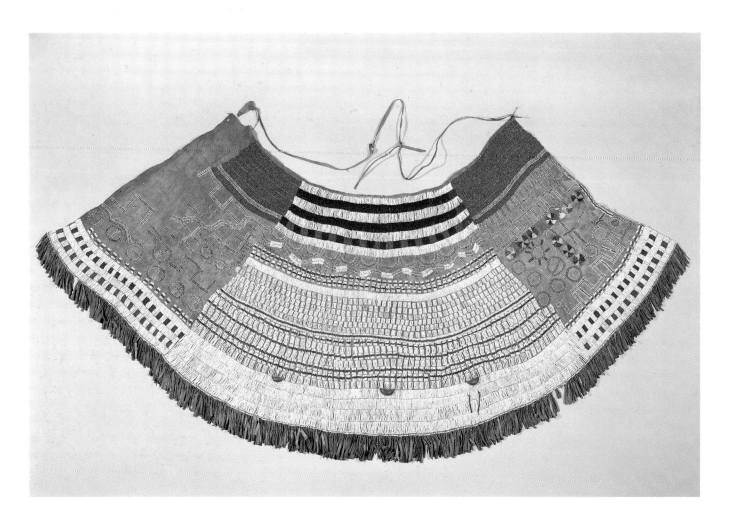

Hide skirt with applied beadwork decoration, Iraqw, Tanzania. Length 25 in (63.5 cm). Commonwealth Institute.

design is a combination of zigzags and circles, the former representing the rainbow and the latter eyes or stars. The deeper meanings of these representations is not known.

Quilting

This is not a technique which is at all common in Africa, but it should be mentioned, however briefly, because it is found widely amongst the people living in the southern Saharan region. Its distribution seems to encompass an area as far east as Khartoum and as far west as the Djerma people of the middle Niger. This may seem an exceedingly unlikely place in which to find heavily-padded and therefore warm garments. It is however, an area which has had an unsettled history, and the padding was not intended as protection against the elements but against arrows and other weaponry. Quilted armour was made by stitching together several layers of locally-woven cotton cloth and was intended for both warriors and their horses. The stitching is frequently carried out so as to give pattern to the garment, and pieces of cloth in one or more colours may be applied to it. The British Museum collection includes a magnificent specimen of horse armour, quilted and decorated externally by patch-worked triangles of red, yellow, blue and black cloth. In North Africa, among the Berbers of Morocco, quilted cloaks worn by shepherds in winter are made by sewing together several layers of cloth.

Patchwork

What distinguishes the technique of patchwork from that of appliqué is the fact that the textile fragments sewn together to form larger cloths are not overlapped, but are

Above Quilted cotton horse armour embellished with patchwork, Sudan. Height 53 in (135 cm). 1899. 12–13. 2.

Right Two Fulani cavalrymen, northern Cameroun. They, together with their horses, are dressed in quilted armour.

Right An Ayt Hadiddu shepherd boy of the eastern High Atlas, Morocco, wearing a quilted woollen cloak to keep out the cold.

Below Men and boys in ceremonial raphia cloth, the one in the middle wearing a patchwork garment with embroidered border, Kuba, Zaire.

stitched together along their common borders. In this sense the term 'patching' as it is commonly used actually refers to a technique which should more properly be classed as appliqué. What we tend to call 'invisible mending' – the attachment of a patch in such a way that no overlap is perceptible – is rather what is implied by patchwork. Amongst the Ganda this is precisely the method used to repair torn barkcloth: a small patch is inserted and sewn to the body of the cloth around the edges of the hole; the patch is then beaten in with the rest of the cloth and, in most cases, the repair is indeed virtually invisible.

The use of a patchwork technique to form a complete cloth is certainly met with on occasion in Africa, though not nearly as frequently as appliqué proper. There is no well-known type of cloth whose conception relies upon patchworking, and the best documented examples come from the Kuba of Zaire. Torday (1910) tells us that the Kuba used to make a type of barkcloth by stitching together small fragments cut to a variety of linear and curvilinear shapes. As we have already seen, barkcloth was used amongst the Kuba in ceremonial contexts and it appears that patchworked barkcloth was the exclusive ceremonial attire of women. However, Torday also collected a number of patchwork cloths composed of small squares of woven raphia cloth. These were made up by attaching alternate squares of dark and natural coloured cloth to produce a chessboard effect. A similar practice of alternating coloured fragments was also characteristic of the patchworked barkcloths. This suggests the possibility that patchworked raphia cloths were intended to fulfil ceremonial functions once performed by barkcloth. Unfortunately, Torday does not record the full circumstances in which these cloths were used though more information has since been published in Cornet, 1980, 1982.

In addition to these examples from the central parts of the continent, examples of West African patchworking are known. One cloth in the British Museum collection includes indigo and white triangles arranged in strips in a fashion which suggests that it is intended to duplicate the patterns found on some tie-dyed cloth. Unfortunately, however, its place of manufacture is undocumented. Some of the Fante *Asafo* flags mentioned at the beginning of this chapter are also made by patchwork rather than appliqué.

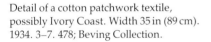

Detail of a cotton patchwork textile, possibly Ivory Coast. Width 35 in (89 cm). 1934. 3–7. 478; Beving Collection.

CHAPTER TEN

EMBROIDERY

Embroidered cotton tunic, Ethiopia, though of Swahili coastal style. Length 42 in (107 cm). Ab. 1.

Finally in this survey of the techniques of embellishing already-woven cloth we come to embroidery, the addition of ornament using a needle and yarn. Some forms of supplementary weft-float patterns have occasionally and mistakenly been called embroidery; and some parts of an embroidered design can present the same effect as supplementary weft-floats: embroidered stitches do, after all, 'float' (except in the case of Kuba cut pile to be considered below). Unlike techniques which form part of the weaving process, however, embroidery is not limited in form by the structure of the ground weave.

The collections of the British Museum contain examples of embroidered gowns, trousers, caps and cloaks from Nigeria, Sierra Leone, Liberia, the grasslands of Cameroun and elsewhere in West Africa, and from Ethiopia. Among the peoples of Zaire, and in particular the Kuba, raphia cloth is embellished with embroidered cut pile. It is, of course, possible to lay in a supplementary weft in the course of weaving in such a way as to cover all or part of the cloth with a series of loops which can then be cut to make cut pile. Pile weaving is an occasional feature of textiles woven in recent years in Nigeria and may be an idea copied from European towelling. However, among the Kuba the pile is certainly embroidered, not woven. Kuba raphia cloths are not, of course, made up into garments comparable with the West African material, either before or after embroidery; this is not the tradition of the area.

Embroidery in West Africa

Embroidery is an art generally associated with the Islamic peoples of West Africa in the sense that embroidery has developed there within the context of Islamic culture. This is not to say that only Muslims wear embroidered clothing, which is certainly not true, although conformity to a fashion for Islamic dress must be counted among the factors promoting the gradual Islamisation of West Africa.

The arts of the Islamic peoples of West Africa have been neglected by Western students. Oriental scholars regard them as thoroughly provincial while many African art specialists do not regard them as art. The stereotype of Islam as a destructive force, and destructive to indigenous African artistic traditions, persists. It is true that Islam has at times discouraged and destroyed representational art, but this is clearly not invariably the case as the discussion of the Yoruba Jubilee cloth above indicates. Why this variation of attitude should exist remains unclear. In any case art does not have to be representational to be 'art', and no artistic tradition is static and unchanging although, in West Africa, we are generally without the information to demonstrate the magenta ground clearly enjoyed considerable popularity at one time. Today machine-spun cotton, rayon and knitting wool are generally used though other materials would still be available.

Heathcote suggests that a structural basis exists for the development of embroidery design given that the simplest, and possibly the earliest, types of pattern relate to particular seams, edges and areas of stress, especially the neck opening and the top of the pocket. The *linzami* and *sharaba* reinforce the neck, which is most under stress, especially if the pocket is filled. The spirals embroidered to the right and back can be seen as proceeding from each end of the *sharaba* while the main elements of the design

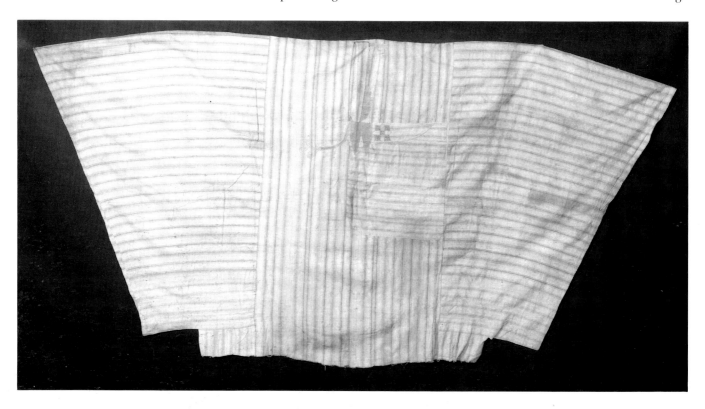

Above Cotton and silk embroidered gown, Nupe, Nigeria. This gown was collected at Egan, a Nupe village on the banks of the middle Niger. It displays the very simplest 'two knives' embroidery pattern at the top of the pocket. Length 50 in (127 cm). 1843. 3–11. 22; The Colonial Office.

Opposite Cotton and silk embroidered gown, Nupe, Nigeria. This gown was presented to a British Vice-Admiral by the King of Dahomey in about 1863. It was presumably made by Hausa (or possibly Nupe) craftsmen. The cloth itself is woven of magenta imported silk with cotton in the warp, and a cotton weft, in strips about 2¼ in (6 cm) wide embroidered with the 'eight knives' pattern. Length 54 in (137 cm). 1920. 2–11. 1.

develop along the top of the pocket and the left of the neck. Embroiderers employ a relatively small number of geometric elements which are put together in various ways, repeated, enlarged, etc. The individual elements are, as might be expected, named and so too are particular combinations of these elements. The long triangular shapes around the neck are 'knives'; a group of five squares is 'five houses'; a pair of interlaced ovals is a 'knot' or a 'tortoise'; a double loop device is a 'sandal'; and so on. Some of the interlacing patterns that are incorporated are very like, and sometimes identical with, the *zayyana* patterns which a Koranic scholar draws on a Koran board as a present for a pupil at the end of his period of instruction. One of the simplest combinations of these elements of embroidery design is called *aska biyu*, 'two knives'; it is made up of two long triangles below the neck, the 'five houses' motif to the left of them and the spirals extending from each end of the *sharaba*. A more elaborate pattern is called *aska takwas*, 'eight knives'. This is probably the most popular of all the embroidery designs and it is certainly the most common. To the *aska biyu* design, three 'knives' are added further along the top of the pocket with three more projecting horizontally from the left of the neck. Down the far side of the pocket turning in towards the centre of the gown, and up over the left shoulder turning again towards the centre, is a series of three or more parallel lines (or bands of interlacing) with three chevrons at each end. The area defined by these last elements may be filled with interlacing and rosette patterns. It is interesting to compare different versions of the *aska takwas* design. In some the elements of it have enlarged to fill the entire pattern area inevitably changing shape or overlapping to accommodate each other. (See Heathcote, 1974, for illustrations of these and other patterns.)

Embroiderers also sometimes embellish the baggy drawstring trousers worn beneath the long wide-sleeved gown. A width of five to eight feet, that is a waistline of ten to sixteen feet, is usual although the British Museum's collections include one pair of trousers with the spectacular waist circumference of eighteen feet! In contrast, the ankles of these trousers are narrow; and they are usually embroidered with a band of some simple design. Around and between the legs of these trousers is often, however, a most extraordinary sight: bold geometric patterns, which include some of the design

Cotton trousers, Hausa, Nigeria. The embroidery is here executed in European knitting wool on 2 in (5 cm) wide strips of cotton cloth. Waist 130 in (330 cm); outside leg 39 in (99 cm). 1966. Af 1. 16; The Church Missionary Society.

by a Mano chief. Schwab adds that the decorations suggest Kisi influence, but does not explain how or why.

Two further distinctive embroidery styles are found on some caps from the western end of West Africa. One is of dyed brown hand-spun cotton cloth with bold designs of lines and squares. This style of hat is made by the Koranko people of Sierra Leone. The other is composed of very finely embroidered patterns on white imported cloth and is from Senegal.

Kuba embroidery

A technique of decorating woven cloth which should be considered within the contexts of embroidery is that known as 'cut pile'. This type of decoration is practised in Zaire and the cloth itself is often referred to in the literature as 'Kasai velvet'. The phrase, however, should not be taken as an accurate description of the historical areas of distribution of cut pile cloths, nor of the nature of the material itself, for it could be misleading on both accounts.

It is certainly true that for the last century or so the manufacture of such cloth has virtually been limited to the Kuba and neighbouring peoples in the Kasai River area. The Kuba themselves have an oral tradition which asserts that their seventeenth-century ruler, Shyaam a-Mbul a-Ngoong, a national hero credited with many important innovations in their public life, learnt the arts of weaving and embroidery from peoples living to the west and introduced them amongst his own people. Oral tradition and documentary history, of course, are not the same thing; it is a mistake to interpret the former as a literal account of past events. Independent evidence in this case, however, suggests that cut-pile cloth was found in more westerly areas, though whether the technique diffused from there to the Kasai is not clear. We know that peoples living within the orbit of the Pende chiefdoms in the Kwango-Kwilu areas

194

possessed such cloth, and certainly its former use is recorded among the Kongo, who, because of their location at the mouth of the Zaire River, had an early and sustained contact with Europeans. Thus a number of examples of pile cloth in use amongst the Kongo were brought to Europe at an early date and some are still preserved, e.g. two in the collection of Sir Hans Sloane by the acquisition of which the British Museum was founded, in 1753. Drawings and sketches made at the time indicate that these cloths were used for the most part in a chiefly context, as clothing, blankets and adornment for the stools and chairs of people with high status. As elsewhere in Africa it was the advent of European trade cloth which conspired to bring about the degeneration in traditional methods of producing and decorating the indigenous raphia cloth. Thus by the beginning of this century the peoples of the Kasai seem to

Embroidered cotton gown, Liberia. Length 35 in (89 cm). 2798.

Left Embroidered cotton gown, West Africa. The embroidery is rendered in red, white and pale blue on a buff-coloured ground fabric, with red felt strips applied around the neck. The place of origin of gowns in this style is unknown. Length 44 in (112 cm). 1934. 3–7. 218; Beving Collection.

Below left The reverse of the gown.

Below Detail of a cut-pile raphia textile, Kuba, Zaire. The thin dark lines are embroidered in the conventional manner. All the yellow parts of the design and the wider areas of black patterning are produced by the cut-pile technique. Width 20 in (50 cm). 1979. Af 1. 2674.

have been virtually alone in continuing the production of the pile cloths. This no doubt is, in part, attributable to the fact that effective contact with the Kuba was delayed until 1884 when the expedition led by Lieutenant Wissmann ventured into the area, though even then the Kuba resisted engaging in trade for imported cloth.

The first real attempt to chart the material culture of the peoples of the Kasai was made by Emil Torday in the opening decade of the present century. The fine collection that he made at the time, which includes a large number of pile cloths, is now in the British Museum, and his account, written jointly with T. A. Joyce, of the methods by which the pile is inserted and the significance of the cloths themselves remains one of the best available. Much of what follows is derived from his observations.

Torday and Joyce themselves used the word 'velvet' to refer to pile cloth. They were not using it in any technical sense but simply as a point of reference in describing the finished quality of Kuba cut-pile embroidery. The base of the embroidery is a square of plain-weave raphia cloth. This may be dyed before embroidery begins or the whole cloth may be dyed afterwards. If the base cloth is dyed in advance the pile may cover only part of the available surface, so that the base colour is visible in places and contributes to the overall pattern. The cloth is sometimes left a natural colour and the whole textile base is covered by pile, and thereby obscured. The thread that is used in the embroidery is a very fine raphia fibre which has been rubbed in the hands in order to soften it and provide the silky texture from which the comparison with velvet

Page 198 Cut-pile embroidered raphia textile, yellow, black and red, Kuba, Zaire. Width 21 in (53 cm). 1948. Af 32. 261

Page 199 Embroidered raphia textile, Bunda, Zaire. Width 40 in (101.5 cm). 1910. 4–20. 408.

Embroidered raphia textile, Kuba, Zaire. Both conventional and cut-pile embroidery are here employed to form the pattern known as *mikope ngoma*, 'the drums of Mikope'. Width 21½ in (55 cm). 1909. 5–13. 544.

derives. The whole cloth can be rubbed in the same way to soften the surface. These variations are to an extent regional features.

The fibres are dyed a range of colours, orange, brown, red, yellow, black and purple, and applied in lines building up blocks of colour to form the distinctive patterns which characterise these cloths. A basic design is rarely worked out in advance and the pattern is simply created from memory in the course of embroidering. All embroidery is the work of women, just as all weaving is done by men (the complete reverse, it will be noted, of Berber weaving and embroidery).

An iron needle is used to insert the threads which are lightly twisted so that they may be easily passed through the eye. The needle picks out one or more of the warps on the base cloth and the thread is drawn underneath the warp and through on the other side so that both ends appear above the surface. A small knife with a specially flattened blade is used to cut the thread so that only a few millimetres remain visible. The process is continued until all the desired blocks of colour to make the design have been applied. Complete cloths are embroidered in this way and also smaller strips which are sewn onto other plain or appliquéd cloths to decorate the edges.

The Kuba also do a more conventional embroidery using an uncut thread, found particularly amongst the Bushong sub-group, and examples incorporating both cut and uncut embroidery are common. The resulting cloth is richly decorated with the unmistakable Kuba pattern types. The Bunda of Zaire also embroider raphia in the more usual way, though the patterns they apply are quite distinctive.

Kuba embroidered designs duplicate those found on wood carvings, in house decoration, body markings and so on. Clearly the resistance offered by the medium in which a Kuba craftsman is working is not considered decisive for means are found to overcome the technical problems in rendering a design on a particular surface, as the long and difficult task of producing even a single pile cloth well demonstrates. This is a clear indication that the patterns themselves have a particular significance and the designs are quite distinctive. The typical form is rectilinear and abstract made up by the intermeshing of chevrons, squares, crosses, and crotchets. A large variety of names are applied to the resulting patterns. A typical selection from the Torday records includes terms such as *Molambo* (the finger), *Misinga* (the strings), *Bisha Koto* (the crocodile's back), *Nyinga* (smoke), *Mikope Ngoma* (the drums of Mikope) and *Woto* (i.e. *Woot*, the name of an early legendary Kuba ruler). There is nothing exceptional about most of these names: they state an observed resemblance between a particular design and a distinctive physical phenomenon; but the way in which a name comes to be attached to the configuration of motifs on any particular cloth is interesting. According to Torday it is the Kuba practice to select one identifiable element in a pattern – such as a particular way of interlocking squares – and apply a name appropriate to this one element to the whole design. The giving of names to patterns, therefore, is essentially a matter of interpretation. Patterns bearing the same name need not be identical and, of course, different people may apply different names to the same pattern. Thus, whilst the innovatory quality of any design may be recognised, one or more pattern names will in virtually every case be available to describe it (Mack 1980).

In all this, however, we should not overlook, as commentators have tended to, what is actually implied in the practice of giving names to patterns. The very activity of naming is an act of classification; it distinguishes a phenomenon as being of one kind rather than another, and it attributes significance. This may seem a trite point to make, but what is interesting about the Kuba case is that they themselves appear to have a clear notion of the significance of applying names. They have an unusually self-conscious attitude to naming and classifying. The classificatory thought of the Kuba indeed has appeared to some commentators so comprehensive, yet tidy – a kind of 'book-keeping', as Roy Willis (1974) has described the categories of Lele thought. The Lele share a common culture with the Kuba. Certainly it is worth emphasising that the classification of patterns is but one example of a careful and orderly habit of mind which is so typical of the Kuba attitude to their material and social world.

The meticulous nature of Kuba thought may also explain a further problem which has already been alluded to; that is, the apparent resistance of the Kuba to the introduction of European cloth. Given the relatively arduous and lengthy nature of the task of preparing raphia cloth, it might easily be imagined that the availability of a ready-woven alternative would have proved attractive. However, when Torday visited the Kasai area in the opening decade of the century he found that European cloth was only beginning to be accepted by the Kuba, but that even then, it was often dyed with tukula (i.e. camwood) to make it approximate to 'traditional' cloth. The first European traders who attempted to establish contacts with the Kuba found that to do so they had to take their trade goods to the east, to the territory of the Luba, where they could be used to purchase slaves, the one trade 'commodity' in which the Kuba were interested. To understand why this should be so we must recognise that the range of cloth produced by the Kuba (plain-weave cloth, appliqué, patchwork, embroidery, and dyed cloth) has distinctive social meanings. Some were worn only by women, some by men, and some on ceremonial occasions, whilst other types were in everyday use; and, as elsewhere, cloth formed part of a total costume which distinguished the social position of the wearer. The use of European cloth, unless invested with some of these meanings, would simply have been anomalous and the initial resistance of the Kuba to its use can be seen as a testament to the comprehensive nature of their classification of textiles.

Raphia textile in the process of cut-pile embroidery, Kuba, Zaire. Sometimes a design is laid out on a cloth in advance using black thread. More commonly, however, the minimum of guidelines are worked out, and as in the present example, the design is built up virtually from memory. Width 25½ in (65 cm). 1979. Af 1. 2678.

BIBLIOGRAPHY

ADAMS, Moni. 1978. 'Kuba Embroidered Cloth', *African Arts*, XII, 1.

ADAMS, Moni. 1980. 'Fon appliquéd cloths', *African Arts*, XIII, 2.

ALLEN, James, de Vere. n.d. *Lamu*, Nairobi.

ANIAKOR, Chike. 1978. 'The Igbo Ijele Mask', *African Arts*, XI, 4.

ARONSON, Lisa. 1980a. 'History of cloth trade in the Niger Delta: a study of diffusion', *Textiles of Africa*, ed. D. Idiens and K. G. Ponting, Bath.

ARONSON, Lisa. 1980b. 'Patronage and Akwete weaving', *African Arts*, XIII, 3.

ARONSON, Lisa. 1982. 'Popo weaving: the dynamics of trade in southeastern Nigeria', *African Arts*, XV, 3.

AUGUSTINS, G. 1971. 'Le Tissage dans la région d'Arivonimamo', *Taloha*, 4.

BAAL, J. van. 1969. *Marokko, Ambachten Handel in een Arabische Wereld*, Amsterdam.

BARBOUR, Jane. 1970. 'Nigerian "adire" cloths', *Baessler-Archiv*, Neue Folge, Band XVIII.

BARBOUR, Jane. 1971. 'The origin of some adire designs', in *Adire Cloth in Nigeria*, ed. Jane Barbour and Doig Simmonds, Ibadan.

BARLEY, N. 1983. 'The warp and woof of culture', *Royal Anthropological Institute News*, 59.

BEDAUX, Rogier and BOLLAND, Rita. 1980–1. 'Medieval textiles from the Tellem caves in central Mali', *Textile Museum Journal*, 19/20.

BEIER, Ulli. 1962. 'Nigerian folk art', *Nigeria Magazine*, no. 75.

BEN-AMOS, Paula. 1977. 'There are three things which are threatening in the palace', unpublished paper, University of Birmingham, Centre of West African Studies.

BEN-AMOS, Paula. 1978. 'Royal Weavers of Benin', *African Arts*, X, 4.

BEN-AMOS, Paula. 1980. 'Patron-artist interaction in Africa', *African Arts*, XIII, 2.

BLOCH, Maurice. 1971. *Placing the Dead: tombs, ancestral villages and kinship organisation in Madagascar*, London.

BOHANNAN, P. and L. 1966. *A Source Notebook in Tiv Subsistence Technology and Economics*, New Haven, Conn.

BOLLAND, Rita. 1989. 'Clothing from burial caves in Mali from the eleventh to the eighteenth century', *History, Design and Craft in West African Strip-woven Cloth*, National Museum of African Art, Washington, D.C.

BORGATTI, Jean. 1976. 'Okpella Masking Traditions', *African Arts*, IX, 4.

BORGATTI, Jean. 1983. *Cloth as metaphor: Nigerian textiles from the Museum of Cultural History*, Los Angeles, Museum of Cultural History.

BOSER-SARIVAXÉVANIS, Renée. 1969. *Aperçus sur la teinture à l'indigo en Afrique Occidentale*, Basle.

BOSER-SARIVAXÉVANIS, Renée. 1972a. *Textilhandwerk in Westafrika*, Basle.

BOSER-SARIVAXÉVANIS, Renée. 1972b. *Les tissus de l'Afrique Occidentale*, Basle.

BOSER-SARIVAXÉVANIS, Renée. 1975. *Recherche sur l'Histoire des Textiles Traditionnels tissés et teints de l'Afrique Occidentale*, Basle.

BOSER-SARIVAXÉVANIS, Renée. 1980. *West African textiles and garments*, Minneapolis, University of Minnesota.

BOSTON, J. S. 1960. 'Some northern Ibo masquerades', *Journal of the Royal Anthropological Institute*, XC, 1.

BOYER, Ruth. M. 1982. 'Yoruba cloths with regal names', *African Arts*, XVI, 2.

BRAY, Jennifer M. 1968. 'The organization of traditional weaving in Iseyin, Nigeria', *Africa*, XXXVIII, 3.

BRETT-SMITH, Sarah. 1982. 'Symbolic Blood: Cloths for Excised Women', *RES*, 3.

BROWN, Charlotte Vestal. 1985. *West African textiles*, Raleigh, North Carolina State University.

BROWNE, Angela W. 1983. 'Rural industry and appropriate technology: the lessons of narrow-loom Ashanti weaving', *African Affairs*, 82 (326).

BRUNELLO, Franco. 1973. *The Art of Dyeing in the History of Mankind*, Vicenza.

BUEHLER, Alfred, BOSER-SARIVAXÉVANIS, Renée and SEILER-BALDINGER, Annemarie. 1972. *Die Textilsammlung im Museum für Völkerkunde Basel*. Schweizerische Arbeitslehrerinnen-Zeitung, Heft 7/8.

BURT, Ben. 1977. *Weaving*, London.

CANNIZZO, Jeanne. 1983. 'Gara cloth by Senesse Tarawallie', *African Arts*, XVI, 4.

CARREIRA, Antonio. 1968. *Panaria*, Lisbon.

CHANTREAUX, Germain. 1941 and 1942. 'Le Tissage sur Métier de haute lisse à Ait Hichem et dans le Haut Sebaou', *Revue Africaine*, LXXXV, 1, 2, 3 et 4 trimestres, Algiers. Société Historique Algérienne.

CHITTICK, Neville. 1969. 'An archaeological reconnaissance of the southern Somali coast', *Azania*, IV.

CLARKE, J. D. 1938. 'Ilorin weaving', *Nigeria Magazine*, no. 14.

COLE, H. and Ross, D. 1977. *The Arts of Ghana*, ch. 4, Los Angeles, Museum of Cultural History.

CORNET, Joseph. 1980. 'The *itul* celebration of the Kuba', *African Arts*, VIII, 3.

CORNET, Joseph. 1982. *Art Royal Kuba*, Milan.

CROWFOOT, Grace. M. 1921. 'Spinning and weaving in the Sudan', *Sudan Notes and Records*, IV, 1.

CROWFOOT, Grace. M. 1931. *Methods of Handspinning in Egypt and the Sudan*. Halifax.

CULLEN, L. P. 1936. 'Barkcloth from Africa', *Natural History*, XXVIII, 4.

DALY, Catherine *et al.* 1986. 'Male and female artistry in Kalabari dress', *African Arts*, XIX, 3.

DALZIEL, J. M. 1937. *The Useful Plants of West Tropical Africa*, London.

DANIEL, F. 1938. 'Yoruba pattern dyeing', *Nigeria Magazine*, no. 14.

DAVISON, Patricia and HARRIES, Patrick. 1980. 'Cotton weaving in south-east Africa: its history and technology', *Textiles of Africa*, ed. D. Idiens and K. G. Ponting, Bath.

DODWELL, C. B. 1955. 'Iseyin, the town of weavers', *Nigeria Magazine*, no. 46.

DONNE, J. B. 1973. 'Bogolanfini: a mud-painted cloth', *Man*, VIII, 1.

DOUGLAS, Mary. 1958. 'Raffia cloth distribution in the Lele economy', *Africa*, XXVIII, 2.

DUBOIS. L. 1951. 'Notes sur les principales plantes à fibres indigènes utilisées au Congo et au Ruanda-Urundi', *Bulletin Agricole du Congo Belge*, XLII, 4.

EASMON, M. C. F. 1924. *Sierra Leone Country Cloths*, London.

EDWARDS, Joanna. 1989. 'The Sociological significance of Mende Country cloth', *History, Design and Craft in West African Strip-woven Cloth*, National Museum of African Art, Washington, D.C.

EGGELING, W. J. 1940. *Indigenous Trees of Uganda*, Entebbe.

EICHER, Joanne Bubolz. 1969. *African Dress: A select and annotated bibliography of sub-Saharan countries*, East Lansing, Michigan State University.

EICHER, Joanne Bulbolz. 1976. *Nigerian Handicrafted Textiles*, Ife.

EICHER, Joanne Bulbolz *et al.* 1985. *African dress II: a select and annotated bibliography*, East Lansing, Michigan State University.

ELLIS, William. 1838. *History of Madagascar*, 2 vols, London.

EMERY, Irene. 1966. *The Primary Structures of Fabrics*, Washington, D.C.

EREKOSINA, J. V. and EICHER, J. B. 1981. 'Kalabari cut thread and pulled thread cloth', *African Arts*, XIV, 2.

ENE, J. Chunikwe. 1964. 'Indigenous silk-weaving in Nigeria', *Nigeria Magazine*, no. 81.

EYDOUX, Henri-Paul (ed.). 1934. 'L'exposition du Sahara', published for *La Renaissance*, XVII, 7/9.

FARIS, J. C. 1972. *Nuba Personal Art*, London.

FORBES, R. J. 1955. *Studies in Ancient Technology*, vol. IV, Leiden.

FYLE, C. Magbaily and ABRAHAM, Arthur. 1976. 'The country cloth culture in Sierra Leone', *Odu*, n.s. 13.

GABUS, Jean. 1955. *Au Sahara*: vol. I, *Les Hommes et Leurs Outils*, Neuchâtel. 1958, *Au Sahara*: vol. II, *Arts et symboles*, Neuchâtel.

GARDI, Rene. 1969. *African Crafts and Craftsmen*, New York and London.

GILFOY, Peggy Stoltz. 1986. *Patterns of life: West African strip-weaving traditions*, Smithsonian Institution, Washington, D.C.

GILFOY, Peggy Stoltz. 1989. 'The eye, the hand and the stripe: North African motifs in West African strip-woven textiles', *History, Design and Craft in West African Strip-woven Cloth*, National Museum of African Art, Washington, D.C.

GOODY, E. N. (ed.). 1982. *From Craft to Industry: the ethnography of proto-industrial cloth production*, esp. chs 1–4, Cambridge.

GOULDSBURY, C. and SHEANE, H. 1911. *The Great Plateau of Northern Rhodesia*, London.

HARTLAND-ROWE, Marian. 1985. 'The textile prints of the Phuthadikobo Museum, *African Arts*, XVIII, 3.

HEATHCOTE, David. 1972a. 'Hausa embroidered dress', *African Arts*, V, 2.

HEATHCOTE, David. 1972b. 'A Hausa embroiderer of Katsina', *Nigerian Field*, XXXVII, 3.

HEATHCOTE, David. 1972c. 'Insight into a creative process: a rare collection of embroidery drawings from Kano', *Savanna*, I, 2.

HEATHCOTE, David. 1973. 'Hausa women's dress in the light of two recent finds', *Savanna*, II, 1.

HEATHCOTE, David. 1974a. 'Aspects of style in Hausa embroidery', *Savanna*, III, 1.

HEATHCOTE, David. 1974b. 'A Hausa charm gown', *Man*, IX, 4.

HEATHCOTE, David. 1974c. 'Hausa embroidery stitches', *Nigerian Field*, XXXIX, 4.

HEATHCOTE, David. 1975. 'Hausa hand-embroidered caps', *Nigerian Field*, XL, 2.

HEATHCOTE, David. 1976. *The Arts of the Hausa*, London.

HEIDMANN, Pierre. 1937. 'Les industries du tissage', *Revue de Madagascar*, Tananarive.

HERSKOVITS, Melville J. 1938. *Dahomey, An Ancient West African Kingdom*, 2 vols, New York.

HODDER, B. W. 1980. 'Indigenous cloth trade and marketing in Africa', *Textiles of Africa*, ed. D. Idiens, Bath.

HODGES, H. 1964. *Artifacts*, chs 9 and 10, London.

HOFFMAN, Rachel. 1987. 'The Fulani *Kerka*: Islamic symbols in a secular context?', paper presented at the African Studies Association 30th Annual Conference, Denver, Colorado.

HUERTEBIZE, G. and RAKOTOARISOA, J. A. 1974. 'Note sur la confection des tissus de type ikat à Madagascar', *Archipel*, 8.

IDIENS, Dale. 1980. 'An introduction to traditional African weaving and textiles', *Textiles of Africa*, ed. D. Idiens and K. G. Ponting, Bath.

IDIENS, Dale and PONTING, K. G. 1980. *Textiles of Africa*, Bath.

IMPERATO, Pascal James. 1973. 'Wool blankets of the Peul of Mali', *African Arts*, VI, 3.

IMPERATO, Pascal James. 1974. 'Bamana and Maninka covers and blankets', *African Arts*, VII, 3.

IMPERATO, Pascal James. 1976. 'Kereka blankets of the Peul', *African Arts*, IX, 4.

IMPERATO, Pascal James and SHAMIR, Marli. 1970. 'Bokolanfini: mud cloth of the Bamana of Mali', *African Arts*, III, 4.

IMPERATO, Pascal James. 1979. 'Blankets and covers from the Niger Bend', *African Arts*, XII, 4.

IMPERATO, Pascal James. 1979. 'Blankets and covers from the Niger Bend', *African Arts*, XVIII, 3.

INNES, R. A. 1959. *Non-European Looms in the Collections at Bankfield Museum*, Halifax.

JACKSON, George. 1971. 'The devolution of the jubilee design', *Adire Cloth in Nigeria*, ed. Jane Barbour and Doig Simmonds, Ibadan.

JOHNSON, Marion. 1972. 'Manding weaving', unpublished paper, Manding Conference, London.

JOHNSON, Marion. 1973. 'Cloth on the banks of the Niger', *Journal of the Historical Society of Nigeria*, VI, 4.

JOHNSON, Marion. 1974. 'Cotton Imperialism', *African Affairs*, 73.

JOHNSON, Marion. 1976. 'Calico caravans: the Tripoli-Kano trade after 1880', *Journal of African History*, XVII, 1.

JOHNSON, Marion. 1978. 'Technology, competition and African crafts', *The Imperial Impact*, ed. C. Dewey and A. G. Hopkins, London.

JOHNSON, Marion. 1980. 'Cloth as money; the cloth strip currencies of Africa', *Textiles of Africa*, ed. D. Idiens and K. G. Ponting, Bath.

Joyce, T. A. 1925. 'Babunda weaving', *Ipek*, vol. I.

Kent, Kate P. 1972. 'West African decorative weaving', *African Arts*, VI, 1.

Lamb, Venice. 1975. *West African Weaving*, London.

Lamb, Venice and Alastair. 1975. *The Lamb Collection of West African Narrow Strip Weaving*, Halifax.

Lamb, Venice and Alastair. 1980. 'The classification and distribution of horizontal treadle looms in sub-Saharan Africa', *Textiles of Africa*, ed. D. Idiens and K. G. Ponting, Bath.

Lamb, Venice and Holmes, Judy. 1980. *Nigerian weaving*, Hertingfordbury, Roxford Books.

Lamb, Venice and Alastair. 1982. *Cameroun weaving*, Hertingfordbury, Roxford Books.

Lamb, Venice and Alastair. 1984. *Sierra Leone weaving*, Hertingfordbury, Roxford Books.

Lanning, E. C. 1957. 'Two bone barkcloth hammers from Mubende, Uganda', *Man*, LVII.

Lanning, E. C. 1959. 'Barkcloth hammers', *The Uganda Journal*, XXIII, 1.

Lavondes, Anne. 1961. *Art Traditionnel Malgache*, Tananarive.

Leib, Elliot and Ramaro, Renée. 1984. 'Reign of the leopard: Ngbe ritual', *African Arts*, XVIII, 1.

Levinson, Rhoda. 1980. 'Lesotho silkscreens and block prints', *African Arts*, XIII, 4.

Liedholm, C. 1982. 'The economics of African dress and textile arts', *African Arts*, XV, 3.

Linton, Ralph. 1933. *The Tanala, A hill tribe of Madagascar*, Chicago.

Loir, Hélène. 1935. 'Le tissage du raphia au Congo Belge', *Annales du Musée du Congo Belge*, série III, III, 1.

Mack, John. 1980. 'Bakuba embroidery patterns: a commentary on their social and political implications', *Textiles of Africa*, ed. D. Idiens and K. G. Ponting, Bath.

Mack, John. 1986. 'In Search of the Abstract', *Hali*.

Mack, John. 1987. 'Weaving, women and the ancestors in Madagascar', *Indonesia Circle*, 42.

Mack, John. 1988. 'De la nécessité naît la qualité. L'évolution de l'art textile chez les femmes Kuba', *Au Royaume du Signe*, Fondation Dapper, Paris.

Mack, John. 1989. *Malagasy Textiles*, Princes Risborough.

Maes, J. 1910. 'Le métier à tisser de la tribu des Akela', *Annales de la Société Scientifique de Bruxelles*, XXXV.

Maes, J. 1912. 'Métier à tisser des Ababua', *La Revue Congolaise*, no. 4.

Maes, J. 1913a. 'Métier à tisser des Batempa, des Bena-Lulua et des Baluba', *La Revue Congolaise*, no. 2.

Maes, J. 1913b. 'Métier à tisser du Lac Leopold II', *La Revue Congolaise*, no. 2.

McLeod, Malcolm. 1981. *The Asante*, London.

Menzel, Brigitte. 1972. *Textilien aus Westafrika*, 3 vols, Berlin.

Meurant, Georges. 1986. *Shoowa Design*, London.

Molet, L. 1952. 'Métiers à tisser Betsimisaraka', *Memoires de l'Institut Scientifique de Madagascar*, I, 2.

Molet, L. 1956. 'Métier à tisser du pays Mahafaly', *Le Naturaliste Malgache*, VIII, 1.

Murray, K. C. 1938. 'Weaving in Nigeria', *Nigeria Magazine*, no. 14.

Musée de l'homme, 1975. *Ethiopie d'Aujourd'hui: la terre et les hommes*, Paris.

Nadel, S. F. 1946. *A Black Byzantium*, chs XIV, XV.

de Negri, Eve. 1962a. 'Yoruba women's costume', *Nigeria Magazine*, no. 72.

de Negri, Eve. 1962b. 'Yoruba men's costume', *Nigeria Magazine*, no. 73.

de Negri, Eve. 1966. 'Nigerian textile industry before independence', *Nigeria Magazine*, no. 89.

Nicklin, Keith. 1977. *Guide to the National Museum, Oron*, Lagos.

Nicklin, Keith. 1980. 'Annang Ibibio raphia weaving', *Textiles of Africa*, ed. D. Idiens and K. G. Ponting, Bath.

Nicolaisen, Johannes. 1963. *Ecology and Culture of the Pastoral Tuareg*, Copenhagen.

Ojo, G. J. Afolabi. 1966. *Yoruba Culture*, Ibadan and London.

Okeke, C. G. 1976. 'Tradition and Change in Igbo Woven Designs', *Nigeria Magazine*, no. 121.

Okeke, C. G. 1977. 'Factors which influenced Igbo traditional woven designs', *Textile History*, 8.

Okeke, C. S. 1980. 'Use of traditional textiles among the Aniocha Igbo of mid-western Nigeria', *Textiles of Africa*, ed. D. Idiens, Bath.

Patterson, R. 1957. 'Spinning and weaving', *A History of Technology*, vol. III, ed. Charles Singer, Eric J. Holmyard, *et al.*, Oxford.

Perani, J. 1979. 'Nupe costume crafts', *African Arts*, XII, 3.

Perani, Judith. 1989. 'The cloth connection: producers and patrons of Northern Nigerian strip weave', *History, Design and Craft in West African Strip-woven Cloth*, National Museum of African Art, Washington, D.C.

Picton, John. 1980. 'Women's weaving: the manufacture and use of textiles among the Igbirra people of Nigeria', *Textiles of Africa*, ed. D. Idiens and K. G. Ponting, Bath.

Picton, John. 1989. 'Technology, tradition and lurex in West African weaving', *History, Design and Craft in West African Strip-woven Cloth*, National Museum of African Art, Washington, D.C.

Plumer, Cheryl. 1971. *African Textiles*, East Lansing, Michigan State University.

Posnansky, Merrick. 1989. 'Traditional cloth from the Ewe heartland', *History, Design and Craft in West African Strip-woven Cloth*, National Museum of African Art, Washington, D.C.

Poynor, R. 1980. 'Traditional textiles in Owo', *African Arts*, XIV, 1.

Rattray, R. S. 1927. *Religion and Art in Ashanti*, Oxford.

Renne, Elisha P. 1986. 'The Thierry collection of Hausa artifacts at the Field Museum', *African Arts*, XIX, 4.

Reswick, Irmtraud. 1981. 'Traditional textiles of Tunisia', *African Arts*, XIV, 3.

Reswick, Irmtraud. 1985. *Traditional textiles of Tunisia and related North African weaving*, Los Angeles.

Roscoe, John. 1911. *The Baganda: An account of their native customs and beliefs*, London.

Ross, D. 1979. *Fighting with Art: Appliqued flags of the Fante Asafo*, Los Angeles.

Roth. H. Ling. 1917. *Studies in Primitive Looms*, Halifax.

Roy, Christopher D. 1982. 'Mossi weaving', *African Arts*, XV, 3.

Russell, T. A. 1965. 'The raphia palms of West Africa', *Kew Bulletin*, XIX, 2.

Sagnia, B. K. 1984. 'Manding indigenous industries: a case study of the historical background, nature of dissemination and production techniques of Manding weaving in the Senegambia region', *Occasional publications of the Gambia National Museum*, Banjul.

Salmons, Jill. 1980. 'Funerary shrine cloths of the Annang Ibibio, south-east Nigeria', *Textiles of Africa*, ed. D. Idiens and K. G. Ponting, Bath.

Schwab, George. 1947. *Tribes of the Liberian Hinterland* (reprinted 1968), Cambridge, Mass.

Seiler-Baldinger, Annemarie. 1973. *Systematik der Textilen Techniken*, Basle.

Shaw, Thurstan. 1977. *Unearthing Igbo-Ukwu*, Ibadan.

Sieber, Roy. 1972. *African Textiles and Decorative Arts*, New York.

SIERRA LEONE, AGRICULTURAL DEPARTMENT, 1929. *Raffia and its Method of Preparation*, Freetown.

SINGER, C. and HOLMYARD, E. J., *et al.* (eds). 1954–78. *A History of Technology*, 7 vols (esp. vols I, II), Oxford.

SMITH, Fred T. 1982. 'Frafra dress', *African Arts*, XV, 3.

STANFIELD, Nancy. 1971. 'Dyeing methods in western Nigeria', *Adire Cloth in Nigeria*, ed. Jane Barbour and Doig Simmonds, Ibadan.

STEINER, Christopher. 1985. 'Another image of Africa: toward an ethnohistory of European cloth marketed in West Africa, 1873–1960', *Ethnohistory* 32(2).

von STRITZL, Angelika. 1971. 'Raffiaplusche aus dem Königreich Kongo', *Wiener Ethnohistorische Blätter*, Heft 3.

SUTTON, A., COLLINGWOOD, P. and HUBBARD, G. St. A. 1982. *The Craft of the Weaver*, London.

TORDAY, E. 1922. 'Notes ethnographiques sur des populations habitant les bassins du Kasai et du Kwango oriental', *Annales du Musée de Congo Belge*, série III, II, 2.

TORDAY, E. and JOYCE, T. A. 1910. 'Notes ethnographiques sur les peuples communément appelés Bakuba, ainsi que sur les peuplades apparentées, les Bushongo', *Annales du Musée du Congo Belge*, série III, II, 1.

TROWELL, Kathleen Margaret. 1960. *African Design*, London.

TROWELL, Kathleen Margaret and WACHSMANN, K. P. 1953. *Tribal Crafts of Uganda*, London.

UKEJE, L. O. 1962. 'Weaving in Akwete', *Nigeria Magazine*, no. 74.

VANSINA, J. 1962. 'Long distance trade routes in central Africa', *Journal of African History*, III, 3.

VERNIER, E. 1964. 'Étude sur la fabrication des lamba mena', *Journal de la Société des Africanistes*, tome XXXIV, fasc. 1.

WEIR, Shelagh. 1970. *Spinning and weaving in Palestine*, London.

WEIR, Shelagh. 1975. 'Some observations on pottery and weaving in the Yemen Arab Republic', *Proceedings of the Seminar for Arabian Studies*, vol. 5.

WEIR, Shelagh. 1976. *The Bedouin*, London.

WENGER, S. and BEIER, Ulli. 1957. 'Adire – Yoruba pattern dyeing', *Nigeria Magazine*, no. 54.

WESTERMARCK, Edward A. 1926. *Ritual and Belief in Morocco*, 2 vols, London.

WILLIS, Revd J. 1885. 'Native products used in Malagasy industries', *Antananarivo Annual*.

WILLIS, Roy C. 1974. *Man and Beast*, London.

Note:

The illustrations, articles and reviews in *African Arts*, a quarterly journal published by the University of California, Los Angeles, are an important continuing source of information.

INDEX